My Bolivian Aunt

Also by Cecil Beaton
The Wandering Years *Diaries: 1922–39*
The Years Between *Diaries: 1939–44*

My Bolivian Aunt

A Memoir

Cecil Beaton

Weidenfeld and Nicolson 5 Winsley Street London W1

ISBN 0 297 00442 5

Printed in Great Britain by
Willmer Brothers Limited, Birkenhead

To
Kinmont Trefry Hoitsma

Contents

Contents

Illustrations

Illustrations except where otherwise credited are by the author.

Author's Thanks

Grateful thanks are due to :-

My cousins, Tecia Fearnley-Whittingstall, Tess Ellert
and Harry Williamson
    for memories revived.

Mrs Beatrice Gausbeck and her sister, Mrs Carmen
Knight-Searles
    for their letters from South America.

Mrs Josephine Alice Jackson
    for permission to quote from the tape recordings of
    her mother, Mrs Alice Lowthian.

Miss M. Bocasoma Bonel and Señor Roberto Querejazu of the
Bolivian Embassy in London
    for information and useful additional material.

Mr and Mrs Philip Ribon, Señor Carlos Aramayo, and
Mrs Hugo Boger
    for their reminiscences.

Mr and Mrs Harding Lawrence and Braniff Airlines
    for their magnificent hospitality in Peru.

Mrs Gladys du Rels Costa of the Bolivian Tourist Bureau in Sucre
    for her hospitality and patience.

Mr Samuel Adams Green
    for his good humour as a travelling companion.

Miss Eileen Hose
    for her kind advice and tireless work.

Miss Sheila Feeny
    for her perseverance at the typewriter and
    always helpful suggestions.

1 Youth

Jessie Leticia was born on January the twelfth, 1864, and was the fourth of my mother's five sisters. The two eldest had disappeared, and nobody knew anything about them or their looks. But the three younger girls were all beautiful. In a family of fine noses Jessie's nose, though perhaps the most perfect, was less nobly pronounced; her complexion was of a veal-like whiteness, her hair of sable, and her turquoise eyes were triangular in shape. Upward-curving little cushions underneath her eyes gave them an enigmatic, or mysteriously amused look. Women who have this 'regard' are very rare and seem always to wield an infallible allure; in the past they have become kings' mistresses. Jessie's lack of height was a disadvantage; but if she was not the most distinguished of the sisters in appearance, she had, from the earliest days, the strongest personality and showed unusual force of character. Nothing daunted her, or quenched her thirst for life; her nature was to laugh and her sparkling spirits bubbled over. As a girl she showed delight in self-adornment, and when she walked along the village green in hats trimmed by herself, she noticed that the neighbours were busy rearranging their curtains.

Ella, Jessie's elder sister, was statuesque with flaxen hair and pale, sad eyes. She married a wealthy man named Frank Williamson of Penrith. Jessie was fifteen years younger; my mother, Esther (or Etty), was junior to Jessie by five years, and Cada by fifteen.

The beauty of these sisters vibrated the village of Temple Sowerby in Westmorland where Jessie's father, Joseph Sisson, had altogether nine children. The two eldest sisters, Sarah Hannah and Mary Jane, it later transpired, had incurred their mother's life-long displeasure by making unsuitable alliances and emigrating to Canada and Australia. They were

never spoken of again. The brothers were also quite anony-
mous. The family tombstones in the churchyard date back for
hundreds of years. Joseph Sisson could be said to be of yeoman
stock, for although his ancestors came originally from Soissons
in France, from whence his name was derived, to settle in the
north of England at Whitehaven where they became lawyers,
his father decided to abandon law for farming, and Joseph also
devoted his life to rustic pleasures.

Joe was a gentle character, thought little about making
money and, although he farmed a few meadows with bullock,
only wished to be left alone to go fishing or to wander over
the fells with his dogs. He did not care for the idea of work but
enjoyed breeding sheep, training sheep dogs, and entering
them at trials. He also enjoyed veterinary experiments –
making up herbal pastes and unguents with which he invented
cures for foot-rot and other diseases common to sheep. He
loved all country trades, including farrier work, and was
pleased when his cart horses needed shoeing. His smithy
became a centre for the village children who watched with
wonder the great bellows, the red-hot iron and the fine horses.
But if Joe Sisson was in a mood to explore the woods, or make
his way down the River Eden, the world and all in it could
go hang.

His wife Elisabeth, born Oldcorne, was extremely beautiful in a healthy classical mould: a Madonna on a calendar with
dark gold, straight hair scraped back from a centre parting.
Her deep-set eyes were piercingly turquoise, and her complexion so daringly red and white that even after death her
cheeks still had the flush of a rose. She seems to have been
a rather strict, ambitious woman with a strong sense of the
various veins in local society. She was extremely particular
about her daughters' friends, and was highly censorious of
her nieces Minnie and Annie, daughters of her comparatively
wealthy brother-in-law Tom, who, although they had been
sent to the expensive school over the border, always spoke
with a Cumbrian accent. Elisabeth could not afford to send her
daughters to the 'young ladies' seminary' in Cumberland which
was only two hundred yards away. Instead they went to the

local 'dame school', run by two old spinsters for the offspring of well-to-do farmers. Here the education was at least superior to that of the 'village school' frequented by the children of farm hands. Elisabeth taught her daughters needle work and how to make themselves pretty clothes. She encouraged them to play Chopin starting off with the left hand, invariably spreading the chords artistically, and smoothing their runs like strings of pearls.

Temple Sowerby is noted in guide books as a 'beauty spot'. Certainly the village has all the picturesque earmarks beloved by the turn-of-the-century painters at the Royal Academy. In high summer the railway station was a bower of roses which, with the honeysuckle and the hay, filled the sweet air with their scent. Past the dark oak woods by the side of a small beck, and an ancient farm at Acornbank named Mill Rig, there was a vast stone which was said to be a meeting place of the Knights Templar, the Knights of the Round Table – from which Temple Sowerby is supposedly named.

'The Cedars' and the adjoining farm buildings, where Joe and Elisabeth lived, faced the village green; the maypole around which the Sisson boys and girls danced with the villagers still stands. The house was small, painted white with a pie-crust-decorated carved porch, and had red blinds edged with lace at every window. Life was extremely pleasant in its quiet, calm way. It was a tremendous event when, during a storm at night, one of a pair of ornamental trees blew down; or, without anyone suspecting it, Mary-Hannah, the tortoiseshell cat, had another litter of kittens in the rocking-chair in the kitchen. When eventually Mary-Hannah had to be given away, she disliked her new home and somehow contrived to walk the forty miles back to her favourite cushion on the rocking-chair.

It was enjoyable to go down past Stye Lane to catch minnows and skim flat pebbles across the deep, dark water of the Scaur, a pool at a turn of the River Eden. Here otters were seen among the red rocks which rose sheer and high and were full of nesting-holes for sandmartins, kingfishers and other native birds. There was fresh excitement when the field by the river was filled with marigolds or with grand mushrooms :

you could fill a clothes-basket within the hour, and then go back and start to pick again. A local farmer gave threepence a pound for the open ones, and fourpence for buttons. If you searched carefully enough in the thickest part of the Stye Lane hedge you might find a hen's nest with several eggs in it. Some hens at the farm belonging to Snickface, a rich and mean farmer with a big nose like a door-snick, would not lay in their own comfortable nests and preferred to hide their eggs in the hedge. Sometimes the Sisson girls returned with an apron full of eggs and laughed: 'Old Snickface would break our necks if he knew!'

Perhaps more than most villages, Temple Sowerby was rich in characters. Living in an old house opposite the church was Old Abram whose sign over the door read:

Abraham Lowthian
Bespoke tailor to the nobility and gentry
for liveries, etc.
Est. since Geo. III.

Old Abram kept a tame jackdaw which used to sit on his shoulder and have scraps from his plate at meals. He was a clever fiddler and played for all the services in the church as there was no organ: a friend played the double bass. His granddaughter, Alice, was the sweetheart of my fifteen-year-old cousin, Claud Chattock, an exceptionally talented pianist with a beautiful voice, who used to sing to her 'The Honeysuckle and the Bee'.

A short way along the village green lived Harry Hubbard, a wizened old man who, with his strong, horny hands, was to be seen stretching the stiff leather that made boots, shoes and clogs.

The Richard Musgraves were at Colgarth, and, until it was destroyed by fire, Lord Brougham was at Brougham Hall. The Murray family owned the legendary Eden Hall where misfortune would follow the breaking of a chalice of engraved glass:

'If 'ere this cup should break or fall,
Farewell the luck of Eden Hall.'

But the great figurehead of the neighbourhood was Lord Lonsdale – known as The Yellow but referred to by lesser folk as Lordie – who looked extremely shabby when he came into Old Abram's shop for some flies, or was seen fishing in the Eden and eating his sandwiches by the river bank. But in other ways he was a great showman. He well knew the effect he created as he sped along like the east wind in his very high landau with two dalmatians running beneath. All the Lonsdale horses were chestnuts, whether for riding, driving, or use on the Lowther farms; his dog-carts, gigs, carriages and family *équipages* were painted bright yellow. Every night he wore a tail coat for dinner with a gardenia in his buttonhole. Lowther Castle was run with a pomp that was considered by some to be excessive and vulgar. A footman stood behind every guest at the dining table as Lordie gave the inevitable toast in the local dialect: 'To the King, to fox-hunting, and the ladies!' Lord Lonsdale was undoubtedly a remarkable sporting character with an uncanny power over wild animals. But locally he was said to be 'not very respectable', and my grandmother would never allow her beautiful daughters to speak to him.

The younger Sisson daughters loved to churn the cream, and help with the jam-making for which they collected the gooseberries and redcurrants from the bushes in the garden and the Victoria plums from the tree on the house wall. None of these large red plums, with the rich mauve mull bloom on the skins, would be eaten as they made such a particularly delicious jam. The ritual was sacred: each plum cut exactly down the seam with a silver knife, the stones taken out and cracked into a muslin bag and boiled in the brew. Then blanched almonds were added to the jars when the steaming liquid was poured in, and finally it was sealed over and waxed. The jam was never opened till the next year's lot was made; but when the jar was undone the scent filled the rooms.

Certainly this jam would have won a prize at the annual Flower and Agricultural Show. From early morning there was a constant stream of every kind of horse going to the show field, as well as cows, calves, bulls, sheep and pigs – all on the hoof, for there were no cattle lorries then. The drovers, mostly the owners of the animals, were in their best clothes with flowers in their hats, and some wore white linen smocks worked in bright colours. By the afternoon all was arranged and set, and the neighbours and villagers, wearing their Sunday best, would arrive in state. The surface of the roads was gritty as they were paved with flint, and the sound of the steel bands on the wheels of the traps rolling over this surface was part of the excitement. Of all the animals at the show the little foals with their velvet noses – but so timid that it was difficult to touch them – were the star attractions; and there was always great rivalry as to who should receive the gold monogrammed card giving the prize for the largest runner beans or shiniest turnips, the darkest plush gloxinias with their white throats, or the fuchsias like Chinese lanterns with shrimps' whiskers. After the results of the Judging Committee had been argued or agreed upon, the rush started for the real farmhouse tea in the big tent: brown, white and cocoanut breads, with every sort of home-made jam, soggy, dark brown gingerbread, gooseberry pasties, rhubarb or apple pies, and huge fruit cakes. By the end of the day all were eaten.

It was an event for any of the Sissons to walk the six miles to Penrith to do shopping, or to go by pony trap or horse sleigh through the snow. Tuesday was market day in Penrith, and a carrier in Temple Sowerby used to take people's parcels and produce there. Sometimes the Sisson girls would go with him, sitting on a bag of meal in the front of the cart. It would take a long while to collect at the various farms, and to pick up the women with their baskets of eggs and butter and crates of hens. The sisters could not decide which sounded the funniest – the hens or the wives.

Occasionally some of the family would prefer to go to Penrith by railway. The train from the Eden valley was a short, jerky affair which puffed hard and stopped short at every station – and sometimes at level crossings – so that the driver could leave a message with anyone he saw, saying: 'Tell our Liza I'll be in for my snip on t'way back.'

Existence could be a bit difficult. The doctor was at best unreliable, and often would arrive quite drunk with an empty whisky bottle in his leather bag. Once under these circumstances he extracted the wrong tooth from little sister Cada's jaw, and on another occasion left her almost to die of diphtheria. Often for two months on end the village could be cut off by snow from the outside world. But provision was made for this at 'The Cedars', and the kitchen ceiling was hung with home-cured hams. In fact all the food on the table was produced and grown nearby, and nothing has ever tasted more wonderful than the night-fished trout rolled in local-grown oatmeal and fried in home-made bacon fat.

Ella, by now resembling a Victorian Mrs Siddons as a rather weary tragic muse somewhat overwhelmed, was looking after her children and three houses in and around Penrith: 'Ferneylea', of a grey Victorian ugliness, 'Sandath House' by the Lake of Ullswater, and 'Lowther Villa', a sandstone Georgian house – with tall windows – in the town. There were house parties with croquet, tennis and boating on the lakes. When Frank, who enjoyed dabbling in all sorts of business schemes, built a flotilla of pleasure steamers, Ella launched the first paddle-boar from Pooley Bridge to Pattendale on Lake Ullswater. When the smaller lakes were frozen the skating scenes resembled Dutch paintings with braziers burning and servants sweeping the snow off the ice. Horse-drawn barouches took picnic parties to favourite haunts. It was only natural that Jessie should spend more and more time staying with her elder sister. Jessie was so full of dash, and had such unflagging zest and health, that she was always the star at every gathering.

But Ella soon discovered that Frank Williamson had inherited, together with his money, the instincts of the gambler. He subsequently won and lost two fortunes. Frank indulged in many far-fetched, romantic financial gambles, and the idea of making investments in Bolivia may well have appealed to him. Could it possibly be in connection with this that Pedro Suarez was invited to stay? At this time my uncle-to-be was associated with many business interests in South America involving rubber and tin, the building of railways in his native Bolivia, and exports and imports. Pedro Suarez had been educated in England where, at Uxbridge School, he had already shown signs of developing into the Latin American Casanova that later he proved to be. The headmaster's daughter became violently enamoured of this oddly dark young giant. She had hopes of marrying him and, when he left to study at the Camborne School of Mines in Cornwall, she peppered him with love letters; these continued when Pedro returned to Bolivia in connection with Suarez estates.

Pedro was an intimate friend of Alfonzo of Spain. One day the King jestingly asked Pedro why he did not buy back his title – to which, in an attempt at wit, Pedro replied that he would accept it only if given to him gratis. But Pedro was proud of his family. He commissioned a Spanish artist to paint an elaborate family tree with the arms of the Suarez de Figueroa from Castile, of whom he claimed to be the thirteenth Count and a descendant of the third Lorenzo Suarez, Count of Romanones.

Lorenzo married Doña Isabella Mejia de Montellegri, a daughter of the son of King Don Fernando, known as The Sainted One. In the sixteenth century another Lorenzo Suarez conquered and cultivated vast inland territories of South America, and founded the city of Santa Cruz. Three hundred years later, several of his descendants left to search for new sources of wealth. Miguel Suarez Arana hacked a road through the fierce jungle to join Santa Cruz with the Paraguay River up to Caceras Lagoon; today this constitutes the most advanced point of the Bolivian frontier with Brazil. Ovidio established one of the first banks, while other Suarez, hearing of the high prices being paid for rubber, journeyed with their entire families and, after great struggles and hardship, opened up to commerce the inaccessible and distant tropical and forested lowlands known as the Beni. Later, they were offered twelve million pounds for their rubber plantations.

Although Pedro's relations owned such vast estates, he did not inherit any great fortune of his own. But he was extremely ambitious and energetic: he had important connections, and was determined to make good – and up to a point he did.

Soon Pedro was back in London where, in 1897, Felix

Avelino Aramayo, whose family had developed great tin mines in Bolivia, became his country's representative. In addition to his ever-increasing business activities Pedro Suarez became military attaché at the Legation.

Pedro had large velvety eyes, thickly lashed, black hair centre-parted, and a Ghengis Khan moustache. A great number of young ladies considered him devastatingly attractive, so he must have exuded powerful animal magnetism. When Don Pedro Suarez arrived in Cumberland at the Williamsons' for a fishing weekend and the triangular eyes of Aunt Jessie fell upon him, she knew she had met her man, and Don Pedro's large heart nearly exploded in response. He immediately broke his association with the schoolmaster's daughter. Later, when he and Jessie married, Jessie was magnanimous enough to send pupils to the discarded young lady who now owned a school of her own.

However, when Jessie announced to her parents that she wished to become engaged to a man considerably older than herself, and a Bolivian to boot, their reactions were in great contrast. 'So long as Jessie is happy . . .' said Joseph as he went off to fish. But we can imagine that Elisabeth, who talked about 'thieving foreigners – you can never trust them!', was utterly scandalized. And indeed, in this Victorian age it was considered quite horrifying for a young English girl to marry a man with a dark vellum skin, and a thick accent that was obviously acquired beyond the Channel. However, Jessie would be the last to pay any attention to such strictures, and she allowed her xenophobic mother no time to make serious objections to her plan. Typically, she had a whirlwind engagement and marriage, then went to London for the first days of her honeymoon. But, unlike her two elder sisters who had been punished for going abroad, Jessie avoided disgrace. She wrote lovingly to her 'dearest of parents with their kind hearts and hands ever stretched for a shelter', and thanked her elder sister Ella for bringing about her present happiness. Her four younger brothers received an assortment of carefully chosen presents, and to her two unmarried sisters, Etty and little Cada, she despatched, from Redmayne in Bond Street, two suits of cloth trimmed with moiré, costing seven pounds a piece. Then she was off with her husband to South America on what turned out to be a very long honeymoon.

It was during the year 1890 that Jessie, in her early twenties, set out for the Beni. Everyone warned her of the hazards of the journey. After travelling by boat and train it would entail scaling and crossing the Andes on a mule (they were surer-footed than horses), lumbering along in a covered wagon drawn by oxen, and shooting the Amazonian basin in a canoe. Certainly she would be visiting places where no white woman had before been seen. Apart from the terror of earthquakes, landslides caused by floods, the menace of disease, poisonous insects, and wild animals, she would be in constant danger from *banderiantes* and savage head-shrinking Indians. But fear was an unimportant element in my aunt's character; neither did physical discomfort mean much to her. Even the worst hardships would be part of this miraculous adventure.

As Jessie and Pedro, an oddly assorted couple, slid smoothly through phosphorescent seas, flying fish leapt, porpoises rolled and gambolled, and the Southern Cross beckoned them forward.

2 Bolivia I

D on Pedro and Doña Leticia, as my Aunt Jessie
was now known by her new relations, arrived in
Bolivia at an exciting time in that country's
history. Wonderful new veins of tin, silver, gold
and copper had been found in the rich, red earth, and the
mining of minerals, together with the discovery of zinc, lead,
bismuth and tungsten contributed to a sudden burst of
prosperity. The first railroads entered the country from Chile
to the mining districts of Oruro and Potosi, from Peru to La
Paz, and new roads and bridges were constructed.

After many centuries of chaotic or despotic rule, Dr
Ismael Montes was to become 'the great President'. With his
progressive liberal government he set about developing the
economy; agriculture and farming were organized on a hitherto
unknown scale.

At a time that has come to be known as the golden era,
Pedro was fortunate in that the President was a loyal and good
friend of his, so that, in conjunction with the delightful family of
Spanish aristocrats, the Aramayos, and the vast branches of his
own family, Pedro had a finger in almost every rich pie. The
Patriarch Francisco de Paolo Suarez of the flowing moustachios, had appointed him a trustee of the export-import firm
of Casa Suarez. On Francisco's death his son Nicholas, a man
of tenacity and courage, who made a fortune for himself in the
remote region of the Beni, was so close a friend of Pedro's that
when Brazil took from Bolivia the territory known as the Acre,
'because the rubber trees were finer,' Nicholas and Pedro together recruited a battalion and fought as best they could in
defence of their country. As a result of his prowess Don Pedro
was made Colonel, and it was as Colonel Suarez that he was
known for the rest of his life.

But the Suarez clan seemed to thrive on family feuds, and

enjoyed keeping up the internecine warfare that periodically exploded into law-suits. It was not to be wondered at that Colonel Suarez eventually found himself embroiled in bitter family hostility.

Don Pedro was understandably proud of his wife and he loved to show her off when they arrived in La Paz. Not only was she particularly beautiful according to South American standards, but she was so spectacular – such a sport. Spanish women were generally kept in the background, and watched the world from behind their wooden *miradors;* but Doña Leticia, in her flowing skirts, highboned collar and large hat, went out with the men, riding side-saddle on her little black horse. She danced and she sang. It was customary in England, at the turn of the century, for dinner guests, if they had any voice for a ballad, to bring their music in case, unexpectedly, they were cajoled strongly enough to perform. Aunt Jessie brought the fashion and her music to the remotest towns. When the carnival season came round, she was the embodiment of gaiety. She became the confidante of numerous newly-found cousins who copied the way she wore her clothes and dressed her hair. She made up her mind to speak perfect Spanish, and she did so in a formal and flowery idiom which people loved. She would never say *'muchas gracias'* without adding *'encantada muy amable',* (*'merci, bien enchantée'*). She was a life-enhancer to a great number of relations in need of a little extra incentive. To Jessie, everything glittered! Everything was gilt! How could she but be impressed by the way gold and silver were lavished indiscriminately on everything. But that the chamber pots were wrought of chased gold – that was too much for her! What a waste! Immediately she put them to an unaccustomed use; they were to be seen, so easily recognizable, to the amusement of everyone from her in-laws to the servants, filled with brilliantly coloured flowers on the chimneypieces. The fires were lit nightly as soon as the sun went down, for even after the hottest sunlight the night air at this high altitude was extremely chilly.

Doña Leticia had been born and brought up in the Church of England, but now she accepted her husband's religion. In turning to Rome she had no self-searching, no misgivings: she welcomed her new religion without questioning. Dogma meant little to her: she was as ingenuous and simple as any peasant woman. Her faith was blind, and this unchallenged, unchallengeable faith gave her great comfort throughout her days.

The gilded rococo churches of Bolivia delighted her with her sense of the spectacular, and the lifelike representations of the sufferings of Christ and the martyrs, and the tears of the Mater Dolorosa, appealed to her sense of the dramatic. She loved the gambolling cupids with their russet cheeks, the blue clouds of incense, and the altars heavy with the scent of tuberoses. With a shawl over her head she prayed with all the fervour of the Spanish.

Pedro's various businesses took him from La Paz to Cochabamba, Sucre and Potosi. Suddenly he would be administering a new railway in some almost inaccessible territory and, in spite of her pleas to go with him, he would sometimes be forced to leave his wife behind in the care of an uncle for as much as twelve weeks. Doña Leticia closed her eyes to anything that others might consider unpleasant. All life had been a holiday to Aunt Jessie, but this prolonged honeymoon was the happiest of all times. Often Jessie prevailed upon her husband to let her accompany him on his ventures; the beauty of the country struck her with wonderment. She could not compare it with her native Lake District. The scale of everything was so vast that she could only exclaim: '*Qué lindo!*' and praise the Creator for the natural wonders of the tropics. She was often thrilled by beauty in things that others did not notice: the pale foliage in the first light, spangled with large crystal drops of dew. She would sigh: '*Qué lindo! Qué hermoso!*' at finding an emerald and green beetle spotted with jet. She became ecstatic at the sight of vast vistas of blue mountains and the incredibly lush green of the fertile plains. She marvelled at the sight of rivers flanked with bushes of sweet flowing broom on whose banks turtles and lizards basked in the heat, and the jungle-forests with willows hanging in garlands from the giant mahogany trees. The fretsaw of speared and spiked leaves, with tall-stalked waterlilies and other grotesque blooms of impossible colours, possessed the same fantasy that Henri Rousseau was painting from his imagination in his Montmartre studio. Even to create such a scene seized him with such terror that he felt he must throw open the studio windows.

But my aunt ignored the dangers. While riding mule-back for months on end she crossed swaying pontoon bridges made of ozier and rope, and although conscious of the tragedy of the San Luis Rey bridge collapse, she considered the hazard only as part of the excitement. Subjected to a sudden thunderstorm, she was as if transfixed by its grandeur; nature even in its wildest forms held no terror for her, but only admiration of its beauty.

Any unforeseen change of plan left her undaunted; a delay of several days gave her the opportunity to explore the vicinity. She became an amateur ornithologist, noting the varieties of different birds: the carpets of brilliant green and yellow parrots, the dazzling colony of egrets (all white), falcons, storks, flamingoes, geese, pigeons, linnets, humming birds, toucans (yellow and red with enormous beaks), and the biggest bird that flies, the condor. She saw bears and jaguars, crocodiles, wild boars, ant-eating ferrets, wild cats, deer and pumas.

It was only natural that any pretty young woman arriving in these distant places, with her newly-acquired, native-born Lochinvar, should be given a great welcome. Often the whole village with its local band was there to greet her. Doña Leticia was looked upon as a beautiful doll with her pink and white Saxon complexion, her brilliant eyes and her rich, silky hair. Friendly Indians took her hands in their dark, primitive paws and stroked them as if she could not be real. Doña Leticia, from the start, showed the qualities that attracted people to her throughout her life; her enthusiasm for everything about her new existence was completely genuine.

Jessie's letters, when, at length, they reached home, were received with astonishment. She had eaten monkey, and guinea pig – much sweeter than chicken. In La Paz they cooked with the dried 'Number Two' of llamas! Each night while

Pedro was away she took a gun and fired it into the sky to frighten away the bandits. 'We fished with dynamite. We let off three *cartuchas de dinamita* in the water with great success. After the explosion eighty fishes were killed.' 'Pedro put two shots in the head of an *auta* (a sort of sea-cow) crossing the river. As it is an animal that has nine lives, it escaped us.'

Pedro's mother, who lived in a small town in the Beni, was said to be ailing, and since it was here that the rubber plantations were bringing in unimagined fortunes to the successful prospectors, it was inevitable that the Colonel must make the long and difficult journey, and his wife was determined that she would not be left behind.

The vast province of the Beni had no roads or railways and could only be reached by river and ox-cart. The dangers of the journeys the Colonel and his lady had so far undertaken were nothing in comparison to those they were now to embark upon. Apart from the wild animals they were likely to encounter, the menace of forays from the unseen savages living in the jungle in huts made of boughs was always present. One of Don Pedro's brothers had been martyred, like St Sebastian, with dozens of arrows, by a wild tribe that he had thought to befriend. Warnings were ignored. The journey was as full of terrors as expected, but at last the two arrived safely.

Life in the Beni was so different from that in La Paz and Santa Cruz that it might have existed on another planet. The change of climate from the heights of the Andes to the tropical lowlands was a shock that took a while to absorb. In this foetid jungle atmosphere where everything grew in such profusion, or on the vast, empty plains, there was scarcely a population. Apart from the Indian natives, and the nomadic tribes without contact with civilization, there were only the newly arrived prospectors who, as soon as they had made their fortune, went away to spend it in Europe. Unlike the nearby Brazilians, who made their rubber fortunes around the port of Manaus and built palaces and an opera house of imported marble, even the rich *Beniarios* lived very simply in barracks and camps made of wood. Since they could only be reached by river, little was brought to them from abroad. *Charki*, beef hung up for days and dried, was the inevitable meat dish; dried leek, banana and yucca the staple diet. The food, cooked on charcoal, was not spiced or heated with peppers; sweet puddings were popular. The more respectable ladies who sat playing bridge, while the menfolk made their fortunes, became enormously fat.

My aunt, perhaps in determination to keep her figure, spent long hours each day on horseback. Once she trotted off, accompanied only by a *peón*, when after some while they came across a herd of wild cattle. Suddenly a bull rushed for them. The *peón* bolted in the opposite direction from Doña Leticia who made for a nearby tree and jumped into the lowest branches; from here she kicked her horse to go home. Pedro, seeing the horse return riderless, sent out a rescue team. Meanwhile, his wife was waiting patiently, and without any fear, on her perch, while the bull continued to circle the tree and paw the ground with excited anticipation.

The stampede for the sudden riches of the Beni produced the inevitable situation that arises when human behaviour is spot-lit under exaggerated, abnormal conditions. The overnight wealth went to the heads not only of many of the menfolk, but of their women too. In the great rush, greed and licentiousness went hand in hand, so that personal relationships underwent severe tests or changes. One of the Suarez contingent married a German-Swiss who wrote a novel about the Beni at this time; but on its publication he was excommunicated from his family clan for having divulged something his in-laws considered 'far too hot stuff'.

Scandal and gossip did not interest my aunt. She knew how to be by herself, with her own fancies and phantoms as companions.

The principal drawback to the Beni was typical of too thickly-wooded, tropical countries, in that enormous mosquitos and insects of all kinds thrive; there are even large bats which suck one's blood while asleep. No surprise then that, eventually, Doña Leticia became ill with malaria, lost a great deal of weight, and agreed to return to England with the Colonel by her side.

Bolivia I

Upon their arrival in Liverpool, with an extraordinary assortment of luggage – including two cages of parrots and sacks of sweet potatoes and oranges – they appeared quite changed; Uncle Pedro was more robust than before, Aunt Jessie weighed little more than a waif. For nearly two years she had to remain in bed. But Doña Leticia's constitution was made, if not of Bolivian gold, then of Cumberland stone. After this time her recovery was complete, and from then on she seemed to be indestructible. She discovered she was pregnant and gave birth to a dark-haired, beautiful boy.

It was now time for the Colonel and his lady to return to Bolivia. Before sailing from Liverpool Aunt Jessie went to say goodbye to her father in Temple Sowerby (her mother had died by now) and proudly to show him her son. Here she summoned the old family doctor to give the child an injection against smallpox. The doctor used a dirty needle, the child caught septicaemia, and died.

3 Beaton Background

My own family, Aunt Jessie excluded, was typical of the Edwardian upper-middle class, and could not have been more English. My paternal grandfather had become prosperous selling timber. He lived in a vast grey mansion, with balustraded gardens and exclamation marks of tall Irish yews, at King's Langley. Here, until the house was destroyed by fire, there were copious gatherings of uncles and nephews, and remarkably hideous aunts and nieces all with guinea-pig faces. After Sunday luncheon everyone was photographed enjoying coffee in wicker chairs among the potted agapanthus on the terrace at the edge of the well-tended lawns. My father, having met the beautiful Etty Sisson while she was staying with her sister Jessie took her to one of those Sunday family gatherings. For once there was something worth photographing. In Aunt Jessie's drawing room, on Christmas Day, my father proposed to my mother while her sister hovered impatiently in the next room to be the first to hear the news. As a wedding present my grandfather gave one of his timber businesses to my father.

My birth took place in a small, tall, red brick house of ornate, but indiscriminate Dutch style at 21 Langland Gardens in Hampstead. Aunt Jessie must have been one of the first people my infant eyes opened upon: as one of my godmothers she vouched for me at the font and lavished me with gifts. From the dawn of consciousness she gave an indication of things that were not part of a nursery routine – that were above the ordinary. For a small boy her world was full of wonders.

As my father's prospects and his family increased, he moved nearer to Hampstead Heath into a vaguely neo-Georgian mansion named 'Temple Court', also of red brick with lots of white paint, its chief assets being that it was light and spacious, that there was a billiard room, and two great oak trees with black trunks in the garden. My father insisted on living in this suburb of London as he considered the air so much healthier for growing children. There were two boys, my brother Reggie being a year younger than me; five and seven years later my two sisters, Nancy and Baba, were born.

We children lived on the top floor where the linoleum-floored corridors were vast and the rooms were airy. The nursery food was always lukewarm and unpalatable, the black skin on the bottom of a piece of plaice being particularly detestable. The children's and servants' bathroom was excessively functional with unpolished wood; if one were foolish enough to confess that one's bowels had not moved for more than a day, the nurse would prod at one's unyielding and most private parts with a barbaric home-made stick of yellow soap.

My mother was calm: nothing except the servants seemed to trouble her. As for bringing up my brother and myself, she did not worry. At an early stage we were told not to giggle while reciting 'Gentle Jesus, meek and mild,' but we were taught nothing of religion, nor of books. We were read aloud to only when ill; the coloured illustrations I saw were the dirty greens and ochres and pinks of the atlas; my mother never took us to museums or showed us picture books; I could not understand my Aunt Jessie's love for the murky urchins or Madonnas in kipper-dark background of Murillo. Nothing was explained. We just slid into life, and presumably we would make our own discoveries. Perhaps this is the best way? And yet . . .

After childhood ended I was never really as close to my parents as I wished to be. My father was always so evasive of intimacy that it was often embarrassing for me to be alone in a room with him. My mother, whom I adored, though much easier of approach and more outpouring by nature, was also, in certain ways, unaccountably retiring and reticent.

One of the subjects that she peremptorily dismissed from the conversation was that of her childhood's home and early family days. With surprising determination she discarded all associations with the past. When a distant relation wrote with a request of some sort, my mother would say: 'I don't know anything about him. We've got nothing to do with any of these people: I don't know who they are.' The possible link to her was a disagreeable one – as if there were a skeleton in the family cupboard. Yet there was nothing of the sort.

Apart from an innate secrecy there was also a family streak of ruthlessness; when one of her brothers made a disparaging remark about her fiancé, Cada, the youngest sister, never spoke to him again. Yet this younger sister, my Aunt Cada, was more forthcoming than the others. She admitted that none of her four brothers ever 'amounted to much'.

My father had been quite a well-known amateur actor playing a variety of parts from *jeune premier* to heavy villain or Lord Augustus in *Lady Windermere*. He kept a book of press clippings and *The Topical Times* wrote of him in *The Man in the Street* by Louis N. Parker: 'Mr E. W. H. Beaton very successfully depicted Jabez Goven, the unshaven, unkempt, untidy, itinerant musician. Beaton, *qui est beau garçon,* completely disguised his identity. He felicitously brought out the traits of the character and was loudly applauded.' In *One Summer's Day* he was 'well cast as Major Dick Rudyard, a part in which there is plenty of "fat" ... the best moment in his performance was the scene with Maysie after the death of Kiddie which received the tribute of tears from a good many eyes.'

When my father married he gave up the stage, but he continued to indulge his histrionic gift for mimicry. Since he was in most ways shy and self-effacing, it was a shock when, goaded on by Aunt Jessie, he embarked upon a full-blooded series of impersonations of actors of the day. His Charles Hawtrey was, no doubt, a brilliant caricature, for it sent Aunt Jessie into convulsions; but his Irving was a quite disturbing experience that shattered the equanimity of this most conventional household. His Herbert Tree as Svengali sent shivers down our spines, and he made terrible faces, dilating his eyes, widening his nostrils, and stretching his mouth to reveal his back teeth. The rasping sounds that reverberated throughout the drawing-room could be heard upstairs, and there were complaints from the nurse that the youngest children had been disturbed by bloodcurdling noises accompanied by raucous outbursts of laughter.

But although the theatre was embedded in my father's heart, cricket was his passion. During the darkest months of winter, his willow would be taken out of the cloakroom locker to be oiled, and the wicket-keeping gloves coated with an orange grease, in preparation for the coming months when his Saturday afternoons and holidays were to be devoted to the game. Much of my boyhood was spent watching what, to me, was always an incomprehensible ritual; perhaps this was the first time in my life that I knew the meaning of boredom. How I would have loved to escape and pay an unexpected visit on my aunt. Her house was not far from the cricket ground. I knew I would receive her usual welcome of screams of delight, and my blood would seem to tingle more quickly through the veins. Unfortunately she was abroad. At the end of the cricket match I enjoyed the damp, wooden odour of the cricket pavilion, and the sweet smell of the new-cut grass in contrast to the rather disturbing sulphurous stink of the old mowings tipped among the nettles at the back. It was always an experience to feel the exploding on the tip of one's nose soda bubbles from a glass of ginger ale given to celebrate someone's having scored a century or a hat-trick.

My mother did not particularly enjoy the company of my father's cricketing friends, several of whom he would invite with a spontaneous gesture back to dinner on Saturday nights. My mother would ask: 'Why did you have to include old Spoffer?' 'Because he appreciates it,' my father would answer. So my mother would pay a thirteenth-hour visit to the cook to order an extra course – a savoury (sardines on toast) – and wander into the garden to add a William Allen Richardson or Caroline Testout to the other hybrid tea-roses in the floating bowl on the dining table.

Within the Beaton family circle my mother was vaguely considered to be 'artistic'. Her clothes were chosen with such an uncanny flair and original distinction; the way she arranged a room, and the delightful bargains she found in an antique shop, gained her much praise, while the hair-tidies she made for charity during her pregnancies showed that she could ring every change in pastel colouring. But although my mother did not show more than a gracious interest in my father's cronies, she seemed to make little effort to cultivate her own friends. It is true that very occasionally there would be a dinner party. Then she would buy a salmon, and long-stalked, heavenly-scented sweet peas for the table centre, and emerald pepper-mints and salted almonds for the silver sweet-meat dishes. But at these 'occasions' the guests seemed quite gratuitous and incongruous for they did not seem to belong to any particular world: certainly the arts or the theatre were not represented.

The months of the year went by with cricket, golf, tennis, billiards and croquet, and riding horseback on the heath. We enjoyed simple jokes and an occasional outing: a picnic on the river at Henley, or a very rare visit to the theatre. I pined to see the musical comedies at Daly's, or the Herbert Tree productions with their elaborate scenery at His Majesty's, but we always ended up at Maskelyne and Devant's at St George's Hall to see, against black velvet curtains, a flight of doves fly out of a conjuror's opera hat or a woman being sawn in half. As a change we were taken to the Golders Green Empire where that boringly wholesome Harry Lauder sang, against a painted background, 'The Bluebells of Scotland'. Roast beef meant Sunday lunch; tangerines, Brazil nuts cut into the shape of a small candle and then set alight, and faces smeared with burnt cork, spelt Christmas time.

It was a blazingly blue-eyed, happy, healthy, respectable household.

4 *West Hampstead*

In 1902 President Ismael Montes had not only appointed Don Pedro Bolivian Minister in London, but Consul-General and military attaché with other official titles. He was also made his country's representative in Paris. Eduardo Aramayo, who was a member of the London staff, recorded in a most detailed journal of his days at the Legation: 'At the end of the *belle époque* the elegant coach, drawn by a team of white horses, in which Don Pedro and his beautiful English wife drove along the Champs Elysées and the Avenue du Bois, attracted much attention.' For both my aunt and uncle the horn of plenty was overflowing. The rubber rush was at its height: money could take them to Monte Carlo, to Biarritz, or anywhere else they wished to go. In Paris they dined at Maxim's, and bought tie pins, brooches and hats in the Rue de la Paix. All Europe seemed one long, big amusement arcade.

Only one great sorrow affected Aunt Jessie: by painful degrees she had come to realize that her husband was not entirely faithful to her. In fact, he seemed to be taking after one of his brothers who, it was said, had been so over-fond of women that he managed to achieve a sort of harem until, one night, the many cuckolded husbands or lovers decided to take their revenge. He was set upon by at least a dozen enemies who with machetes, axes and sticks, bludgeoned him, long after his scalp was split open and his brain sent flying in all directions. However, his brother's terrible end did not deter Pedro. But Aunt Jessie never questioned the wisdom of her choice of husbands; she knew Pedro loved her and in her eyes he could do no real wrong.

Don Pedro's sudden importance caused jealousy among his staff, one of whom said it seemed as if Bolivia and its Treasury had no one else, or the funds, to fill these positions.

Uncle Percy named No. 74 Compayne Gardens, his house in West Hampstead, 'Santa Cruz', and with his wife entertained a constant flow of fellow diplomats, and an amorphous crowd of every sort of South American. My aunt had invited my mother to come from her village home to enjoy the gaieties of the town, one of which was a visit to see an amateur company playing in *A Bunch of Violets*. My father was the male lead. When the two met it had been a question of instant love, and it was from 'Santa Cruz' that the wedding invitations, printed in silver, were issued for the nuptials on 7 March 1903.

My first conscious memories of Aunt Jessie are her cascades of musical laughter; her gaiety warmed every cockle of my childish heart. She was slightly plump, her hair was a rich mahogany, she wore lots of jewellery and was gaudy and grand. She seemed to be in a perpetual state of euphoria. Of necessity one's parents must imbue a sense of discipline into everyday life; Aunt Jessie broke many of the rules and showed us the rare and the special. 'Now you mustn't spoil them, Jessie,' my mother implored. But my younger brother and I loved being spoiled by her.

As an early birthday treat for me, she organized an entertainment of juggling and horse-play by three white-faced, elderly clowns. I can still remember the strangeness that I then felt watching these rather sinister and fantastic antics against the dark setting of my aunt's dining room. The small red eyes and the dots of black paint on those white mask-faces perhaps gave me my first glimpse of the world of make-believe. I couldn't have been more than two and a half years old.

Aunt Jessie's food was always so much more romantic than our nursery fare – either piping hot and spiced, or frozen like snow. She introduced us to olives, *marrons glacés*, and wild strawberries with sifted sugar and slightly sour cream. She always treated us to an extra bit of forbidden plesaure, and let us peep into the delights of an adult life – the most exciting thing a child can know. Children often enjoy luxury more than grown-ups; they can be far more worldly. Here, perhaps, in my aunt's surroundings, I formed what Adler would call my 'life style'.

Aunt Jessie's manner was extremely 'Continental'. Her eyes were over-active and she would cast them up and down and around a room as she waved her hands in the air. Then in mid sentence she would say: 'What isst that word is for "tarhr-ran-tulah" – that thing with eight legs covered with long hair?' Her voice was sometimes sonorously deep, and when she exclaimed in pleasure or wonder, or when she had occasion to call someone, it became almost exaggeratedly musical. Like everything about her, except her physical stature, her ways of speech and her manner, like that of a born actress, were over life-size.

Her narratives were sprinkled with the most romantic-sounding names and she would enjoy giving a succulent emphasis to each distinct syllable: Valparaiso, Lima, Iquitos, Arica, La Paz, Potosi, Cuzco, Cochabamba and Sucre became tone poems so little resembling the sounds that were familiar in our nursery. Oslo, Riga, Alabama and Mobile, from whence my father, on timber business, sent us postcards, were the most exotic sounds we could produce, while more frequently used in our daily conversations were Birmingham, Cromer, Reigate, Margate and Golders Green.

Not only was Aunt Jessie's conversation peppered with foreign words and phrases, but she had a very un-English accent. Her peculiar-looking husband Pedro, our Uncle Percy, was 'Peth-er-orh' to her. She pronounced potato 'pott-att-tohh', and tomato 'tomm-art-tohh'. Instead of swearing she used a Quechan expression: 'Orch-ta-taie!' or would emit little foghorn cries of 'Tutte, tutte, tutte,' 'Scissors, *will* you cut!' or 'Orh, rotten cotton!' Perhaps she invented certain expressions, for I never heard other people describe something negligible as 'so much nothing', or 'it is and it 'tissn't'. 'Orh, let him get on with it,' and other 'Aunt Jessieisms' were to become part of our vocabulary.

Even at a very tender age I realized that Aunt Jessie was never quite taken seriously by my family. We all referred to her with a smile on our faces; she was a comedy character: a bit cracked. 'Oh, that's just Jessie at her tricks!' 'That's another of Jessie's nonsenses!' 'Have you heard the latest? Aunt Jessie is having tennis lessons.' 'Aunt Jessie has started to read fortunes from the palms of your hands.' 'Aunt Jessie has begun to have her voice trained.' (Even I could tell Aunt Jessie had no ear and sang flat.)

Aunt Jessie had pets: a small Yorkshire terrier called Tiny with many gold medallions hanging from its collar, and a black Pomeranian named Ronnie. Generally hidden for warmth in her Chinchilla muff was a chihuahua dog that was like a silk black spider with curly tail, spindly legs, and enormous protuberant eyes. On one of my aunt's shoulders Chilla, a minute chinchilla marmoset, sat chattering.

Then Aunt Jessie added a red squirrel to her collection of pets. 'Dirty little thing!' said my mother. 'But no,' said Aunt Jessie, 'it's a little darling, is Tango,' baptised in the fashion of the time before the First World War – and the squirrel immediately dropped a few little pellets from its mistress's shoulder. Tango was a wild and wonderful creature to which eventually I fell heir. Whenever I let him out of his cage he imagined himself free in the jungle of Ithatos. Tango gave a new dimension to my bedroom by leaping from the picture-rail to the pelmet-boxes above my windows, and thence on to the overmantel above the chimneypiece. I still savour his warm, musty smell, and in my inner ear hear his chattering, tapping sounds as he cracked the shells of nuts. But one day Tango escaped into the garden, tree-hopped to Hampstead Heath, and never came back to captivity.

Uncle Percy, when I first saw him, was a vast, grey-faced, cinder-haired man with enormous moustachios which were then waxed at the ends and turned up into long, pointed spikes. His sepia eyes had primrose whites; his unusually large and much-displayed tongue always seemed extremely dry: his sub-basso voice sounded as if it needed oiling. He spoke English with a strong accent and delivered his lines in a measured manner. As he stretched his mouth at the corners before opening it wide to admonish 'Chesshie' for some extravagance of behaviour, the effect was extremely comic.

He had a quiet, restraining influence upon my aunt if her exuberances were likely to go too far; but although he did not smile, or laugh, at her follies, he never became out of patience with her. He was neither moody nor bad-tempered. I doubt if he ever uttered a cross word – except to his valet, Arturo, when he found, at the last moment, that his court uniform had become too tight. To my brother and me he appeared courteous and dignified in the extreme, but was sufficiently enigmatic in his avuncular way to fill us with a certain awe.

My father had a whimsical sense of fun. He thought it would be an amusing way of informing my Uncle Percy, who no doubt was lacking in humour of any kind, that my mother had just given birth to her first daughter if I, at the ripe age of five, were to telephone the news to him. The telephone, although still quite an innovation, had, for some time, been in use at 'Santa Cruz', but only just recently had one been installed in the library at 'Temple Court'. My father gave the operator the number he wanted, then lifted me on to a stool in order that I could speak into the mouthpiece while I held the receiver to my ear. In response to a muffled grunt at the other end of the line, I squawked in a piping voice: 'Uncle Percy, Uncle Percy, Mummie's just had a little girl.' I could not quite understand Uncle Percy's surprised reactions. More shrilly I gave the same information. Once more I was baffled. Defeated I handed the earpiece to my father. He spoke into the mouthpiece and, after a short *pourparler,* I heard him say : 'Sorry, it must be the wrong number.' Children can be just as embarrassed on occasion as grown-ups; the whole of my face and neck became suffused with scarlet.

Eduardo Aramayo wrote of his Minister in terms of admiration; he described him as a good, affable friend, methodical in his habits, very much given to mysticism and philanthropy. 'He was tall and imposingly military, creating a great effect when he appeared with the constellation of decorations, which were the most effective credential of his noble acts, spread across his broad chest.' Señor Aramayo made reference to his peculiar, monotonous, toneless voice. He considered that my uncle was often badly advised by his lawyers and embarked upon risky speculations in which he lost heavily. He was often surrounded by pleasure-loving people who exploited his childish vanity and encouraged him to give ostentatious parties at the best restaurants where he was possibly the one who enjoyed himself least. 'He did not smoke or drink, although I heard it said, whether or not it was so, that he was only temperate down to a certain region of his body.'

Señor Aramayo, however, was of the opinion that, all in all, my uncle 'did much honour for Bolivia', and that his wife knew more than many Bolivians of the fantastic and dangerous jungle and rapids of the Amazon River, where she gathered unforgettable experiences which she recounted with great enthusiasm in such correct Spanish that one could never have guessed she had learnt it in those solitary places.

Obviously Uncle Percy shared the general admiration for his wife. He knew her to be the most fascinating and desirable of all women. Look how beautifully she was dressed! Her hats alone caused a sensation in London – though they were difficult to manoeuvre whenever she went out in her open carriage. When Welby, the driver who now became chauffeur, appeared at the wheel of the new Sunbeam with its canework body, lots of highly polished brass-fittings, and an inconveniently low roof, the situation became even more fraught. Welby always appeared as if it were a treat to do my aunt's bidding; in fact her good-humour was reflected in the shining faces of all her servants. Even the distinguished, grey-haired butler wore a perambulating smile. Perhaps the greatest character was Arturo, a native of the Beni, small, very young, nut-brown and ugly. At first Arturo did duty sitting beside Welby, leaping down when his master and mistress arrived at their destination to open, very ceremoniously, the coach door. Arturo was inordinately proud of being allowed to perform the same service from the Sunbeam. Arturo was then taught how to look after the Colonel's dove-grey morning suits and the uniforms. When he grew up he helped to wait at table wearing a livery of the Bolivian colours: red, yellow and green. The butler died unexpectedly and Arturo took on those important extra duties too. Like most of the Suarez servants, he remained forever faithful. The excellent cook, Sarah, was English and an intrinsic part of the Suarez household. She was impeccably

clean and old-fashioned with her hair scraped up into a Dicken-
sian wooden topknot. She was delighted when children came
into the kitchen and stole her coconut cakes. There was never
a question of the head housemaid, Ella Mutlow, and her
second-in-command Edith, or even the scullery maid, ever
giving notice. Marthe, my aunt's lady's maid, continued in her
devotion long after the day misfortune struck.

From my earliest days it was always a particular treat to
go down ('nearer to town') to 'Santa Cruz'. Inside the railings
a small courtyard of large black and white marble squares led
to a Swiss portico. The house behind this curious excrescence
was built in the 1880's in no known style, and in comparison
to 'Temple Court' seemed so mysteriously dark. It savoured
of a hot-house atmosphere. The walls of the hall were of sombre
olive, the furniture ebony, and banisters of heavy chestnut.
Thick lace curtains shrouded the windows, and every room
seemed draped as if in an attempt to keep at bay the tropical
heat outside. A flight of stairs led to a tall window of thick
and oily stained-glass on the landing; from here a discreet
veneered door opened into a lavatory. To enter this little chapel-
like sanctuary was an awe-inspiring, yet delightful, experience.
In a hazy, ecclesiastical light, seeping through a green and
yellow glass window, one walked upon thick Turkey carpets
towards the throne chair placed at the top of three carpeted
steps. The toilet seat was of mahogany, the china pan beautifully decorated with water-lilies. Instead of pulling a chain one
lifted a brass-ringed handle; the ensuing flush was discreetly
silent.

The engraved glass windows of Aunt Jessie's bedroom
gave on to the front of the house and cast pools of light upon
the ruby and purple patterned carpet. The room seemed very
large and was filled with over-size furniture: a meandering
brass bed, a huge cheval glass, triple mirrors, and heavy,
mirror-fronted wardrobe. Everything she possessed seemed so
different from anything that we had at home. It was the greatest
pleasure to go into her dressing-room and rinse one's hands at
her marble-surrounded wash-stand. Here the basin was
decorated with blue iris, and the soap was of a dark red trans-

parency with a subtle scent – so unlike that other hated yellow carbolic soap at home. Even the household commodities possessed their own fascination. Although my aunt's bedroom was always kept at an invariably gentle temperature, in addition to the general heating system a handy portable electric stove was strategically placed. The copper casing, with a boldly simple art nouveau design for its handle, contained three large, upright-standing sausages made of frosted glass. Before they were switched on, they reminded me somehow of the bladders from the clowns' shop in the harlequinade after the pantomime, or the aqualungs which deep-sea-divers wear today. But when the stove was in use, the sausages became suffused with a brilliant, apricot glow and extended a benign and never scorching heat. It was a magical object, and it was typically hers.

Uncle Percy's bathroom was magnificently equipped with mahogany-surrounded bath with heavy gold taps, elaborate weighing machines, and electrical appliances for keeping his figure within bounds, and for preserving his hair. While making his ablutions and shaving he wore a net tied behind his ears to cover his moustache, and he had his own special drinking cups with an extra lip to prevent this great ornament being in contact with his tea or coffee.

Apple-green silk covered the walls of Aunt Jessie's drawing room. Upon them hung an extraordinary collection of too-elaborately framed plaques of painted porcelain. A tall, glass-fronted cabinet of shining marquetry imprisoned every sort of china ornament – no doubt mostly gift horses. A grand piano was covered with an embroidered and bobble-fringed brocade cloth on which stood a platoon of relations in stiff court dresses and uniforms. The furniture was extremely formal with 'French-style' chairs placed, like islands, about the room while others lined the skirting boards. On the scrolls, arabesques and volutes of the champagne-coloured carpet stood five-foot-tall, trumpet-shaped glass vases sprouting fronds of pampas grass: the gilt *jardinières* overflowed with the inevitable palms. Someone had always sent a florist's arrangement of azaleas and mixed ferns in baskets with thanks for some hospitality received.

Even as a child I realized how unlike most other well-to-do houses, with their floral chintzes and chaste-coloured taffetas, this hotch-potch was. Here nothing was pastel-coloured, or of 'old rose'; no spindly, fruit-wood suites upholstered in watered silk, but I loved my aunt's overflowing exuberance.

The dining room was dark and rich but not melancholy. Over the vast expanse of polished table hung a gilt lighting fixture with green, pleated silk shade, heavily fringed; this could be raised higher or lower by a pulley. Under it, at meal times, a massive epergne was flanked by an elaborate array of heavy silver candelabra. Strategically placed were embossed silver dishes for crystallized ginger, dates, and candied violets. The red and green wine goblets were of cut glass. The walls were of alternate stripes of shiny and matt Regency green. One wall was almost entirely taken up by the gargantuan sideboard on which mangoes, custard-apples, peaches, and other luxurious fruits were displayed in gold baskets tied with satin ribbons on heart-shaped handles. The opposite wall consisted entirely of windows giving – via many layers of velvet and Nottingham lace – on to an iron verandah which overlooked the garden where a marquee seemed always to be in the process of being erected or taken down.

On the level of the garden, at the back of the house, was the large aquarium-like playroom-grotto. Shadowed by the iron balcony and the steps leading from the dining room above, it was made even more darkly mysterious by being painted in subaqueous green. Bears and tigers with glass eyes were made into rugs that lay around the floor, and stuffed birds and fish with histories stared out of cases on the walls.

It was here that I heard grand opera for the first time. Aunt Jessie had a phonograph, a curious gramophone with – unless I am mistaken – cocoa-coloured cylinders of metal which gave forth blurred, scratchy reproductions of the ghostly voices of the past. My aunt would hark back to the glory of Covent Garden on Melba nights, or the gala performances for visiting Royalties when the fringed white satin programmes, here preserved, bore the names, printed in gold, of one more memorable perfomer after another. I relished her descriptions of how all the boxes, bedecked with wired carnations, were filled with men shining with orders, or women whose diamonds glittered whenever they fidgeted. My aunt also had another gramophone with shiny black records. But from the tortured sounds issuing through the large convolvulus-shaped horn, I could not appreciate the cult for Tetrazzine singing 'Io Sono Titania' or arias from *Manon* and *Traviata,* for Patti straining her vocal chords as Lucia, or Caruso about to burst during 'La Donno E Mobile' or 'Vesti La Guibba'. Listening to this curious music I did not expect that, one day, I would find great happiness in working in the realm of opera design.

This strange, cavernous room provided the setting for another initiation – namely my first sexual experience when, to my utter bafflement and surprise, I was seduced under the billiard table by an elder cousin.

On rare occasions, from the mahogany door at right angles to the dining room the giant figure of Uncle Percy would slowly and quietly emerge. He appeared like a well-behaved orang-outang. Through the darkness behind him I could dimly see his dark, jungle-green study. It was an impressive, even formidable eyrie, with huge roll-top chestnut desk, green china-shaded lamps, piled boxes of files, and a ghostly clerk with pale, mushroom face blinking in the gloom. There was no question of going into this forbidden Holy of Holies: even Aunt Jessie would not have been allowed to 'spoil' us to that extent. One wondered what went on in there. Probably nothing more important than the sending-out of pasteboard cards inviting friends to Madame Suarez's supper party at the Carlton Restaurant on Thursday, 12 June.

At Aunt Jessie's there was always a great activity: the house was never empty. A Sister of Mercy was sitting in the hall about to receive some benefice, or two ugly nuns, wreathed in smiles, hurried down the stairs with a filled collection box. At least one dark-haired young man would be staying in the guest rooms, or the Williamson nephews – now orphans – would be harboured in their adopted home for the holidays.

Bells always rang; strangers and packages arrived: it seemed as if there were always preparations for a party.

Each morning Uncle Percy would walk to the nearby church, then, having said his prayers – and perhaps having confessed his latest adulteries – he would be driven by Welby to the Consulate in the city.

Apart from watching from the office windows the Lord Mayor's procession there could have been little excitement in the Consulate, for ties between Bolivia and Great Britain were simple and friendly. A few years earlier they had not been so: in fact, relations had been completely interrupted. The legend ran that the British Minister in La Paz, accused of taking part in a conspiracy against the government, had been put on a donkey, and ridden out of town. When Queen Victoria heard the news she is said to have commanded: 'Bombard them with shells.' But when told that this would be impossible since Bolivia possessed no coast, she imperiously crossed the country off her map.

So my uncle, having determined the political destiny of Bolivia for a few moments each morning, would then turn his interests to the Casa Suarez or the rubber business in the Beni. It was Uncle Percy who arranged to lay the whole of the Savoy Hotel forecourt with Parar rubber in order to allay the noises of the carriages bringing the privileged to the hotel. Nico Suarez's interests and estates needed constant attention, yet Uncle Percy had time enough in which to amuse himself.

That 'Peth-er-orh', even in the face of his wife's growing displeasure, should continue his sexual indiscretions, may be put down to some urge stronger than he could control, but that he should not have tried to hide these exuberances from his wife seems quite extraordinary. Incredible as it may seem, in a wild moment of uncontrollable passion, he suddenly attacked my mother in his dining room. But the force with which she threw a heavy bunch of keys in his face stunned him, and was in fact so great that they ricocheted on to the mahogany door, where the marks and scratches remained a lasting taunt to his shame.

It is possible that, while on his travels in Bolivia, Uncle

Percy had been pricked by a thorn of the jatropha bush, for it was said to be an aphrodisiac that induces the wildest impulses. It was of constant distress to my aunt that 'Peth-er-orh's' greedy eyes fell upon many a pretty woman's unadorned bosom and that he would immediately proceed to do something about it. My aunt no doubt created many scenes of outraged indignation – the one advantage being that, in order to assuage her, my uncle would offer his wife a replica of the plastron of diamonds he had given to his latest favourite. But once this fatal disposition of my uncle turned into a tragedy. Don Pedro became more than a little attracted by a friend of my aunt 'whose name shall remain unmentioned'. This handsome woman had two equally good-looking daughters who equally fell under the lure of their mother's lover. My inexhaustible uncle responded warmly to all three; but when one of the daughters, said to be the most beautiful, discovered the situation, she committed suicide by throwing herself off a precipice.

There is no doubt but that behind locked doors there were violent altercations between my aunt and uncle. However, Jessie must have learnt that South American men were in many ways unlike European husbands, and that it did not mean that her Pedro loved her any the less if he could not resist a few little peccadilloes on the side. In spite of increasing girth and greying hair Don Pedro continued to attract a great number of women. Aunt Jessie was not one to fret: she decided to forgive and forget. When she reappeared from some *sub rosa* scene, resulting from her latest discovery, she played her role with complete authority, and the tears only tightened her cheeks and made her eyes all the brighter.

It was quite natural that Aunt Jessie was never lacking in admirers. 'That poor Captain Beddington looks so love-lorn,' people would whisper. But though her manner may have been flirtatious, she was absolutely faithful to 'Peth-er-orh'. 'I know what's what,' she would say. Her gaiety and contralto sympathy endeared her automatically; with no conscious effort she attracted people to her, and friends clustered round her greedily. She did not disappoint them: they were never given an 'off' performance – she was always game and willing to participate. Not only was she a special delight to all children, but to children of all ages; she brought out the child in even the elderly.

Aunt Jessie herself had no wit; she never made an aphorism. Yet she was surrounded with laughter. This derived from her ever-youthful joyousness, zest for life and sense of its funniness. She could see the humour in any situation, especially if she were personally involved; she was always the first to laugh at herself.

On certain formal occasions, and particularly when Don Pedro was standing by, at attention, it was necessary for her to appear extremely serious. Although her look might be one of assumed wistfulness with raised eyebrows, if she recognized a twinkle of dangerous amusement in anyone else's eye, she might give them a collusive smile, then gradually become convulsed and, if the occasion allowed it, would throw back her head and let forth a marvellously infectious roar. Perhaps it is the fashion for women to laugh less today – perhaps there is less for them to laugh about – but, on most occasions, any room that Aunt Jessie graced would soon resound with her deep-hearted peals of merriment. These would be taken up by the others, and only the gentle, restraining influence of Uncle Percy would bring a little calm to the scene.

Perhaps it is a Latin American characteristic to play extremely simple jokes on one another. 'Oh, I'll get even with you for that one!' someone would warn a friend who, in January or June, had been made an April fool. Newcomers from Bolivia were not exempt from the ragging, and one young man, who knew very little English, asked what he should say to the taxi driver who had brought him to Compayne Gardens. The answer given and duly repeated was: 'What's the big idea?' Such was the commotion outside 'Santa Cruz' that Arturo had to run down the black and white steps to placate the angry driver. Discreet coughs, or explosions of suppressed laughter, greeted a lady with gooseberry eyes peering through thick glasses, named Peneranda when, asked about her husband, she replied: 'She's very well now, thank you; but she was so ill with her rheumatism that she had to stay in La Paz. She join me here later when she come over with my sister and his husband.'

The reasons for being so readily amused by Aunt Jessie's antics were various; perhaps one was her innate lack of facility. She did not possess a natural fluidity of movement or an intrinsic grace; there was nothing quick and erratic about her: everything was measured. When she lit a cigarette it was with intense deliberation; no expression on her face was non-committal, no gesture off-hand. She gave the impression that any move that others made quite instinctively had to be learnt by her: thus everything became quite an amusing adventure of perseverance. Even when we children first knew her, the fact that she was not only slightly *potelée,* but extremely small, added piquancy to her every step and gesture. One small foot forward, step down, and now the other . . . 'Aunt Jessie's taking a hot bath' conjured up an amusing picture because one knew that she would put her little big-toe into the bath very gingerly, and that when she realized and approved its temperature, she would, after many manoeuvres, lie back in a state of beatitude. One knew also that she enjoyed with an extraordinary keenness every variation of sensuous feeling provided by the hot and cold taps.

When she swam in the sea you knew she had been carefully instructed: 'In – wide – close,' and was remembering every aspect of her lessons. Another trait which not only caused amusement but also deep respect, was the fact that she never took anything for granted. Every action, or reaction, was as if she were experiencing something for the first time: she was a pristine gauge. No one appreciated more the flavour of a new-laid egg fresh from the nest; when she put a spoon of cream into her mouth it was as if she had not tasted such richness; when she buried her face in a clump of cowslips it was as if she had never before known their scent.

It was perhaps significant that although she was impressed by the exoticism of the orchids and other tropical waxen blooms of the Beni, and was in full admiration of the expensive flowers that were sent by rich South Americans from the best London

Group outside the conservatory at Ferneylea, the Cumberland home of Ella Williamson taken in 1889 at the time of Jessie's engagement to Pedro Suarez. Left to right: Frank Williamson with his son Frank, my Aunt Jessie, Uncle Percy, and my mother, Etty Sisson.

Jessie's father, Joseph Sisson, at The Cedars,
his house on the village green at Temple Sowerby, Westmorland,
at the end of the last century.

Jessie Suarez (standing) with her sister Etty
and her father Joseph, in mourning after the death
of my grandmother Elizabeth.

*Esther (Etty) Sisson, at the
time of her engagement.*

Ella Sisson.

Jessie Sisson, before her marriage.

On the lawn at Compayne Gardens: group including Aunt Jessie
(holding my brother Reggie), my mother,
Aunt Cada and her husband Richard Chattock, and myself (centre).

My brother Reggie, myself (centre) and Aunt Jessie on the steps of
'Santa Cruz' in Compayne Gardens, in 1908.

florists, she really preferred English wild flowers to any others. And somehow she had a way with them. She would return with an armful of sagging bluebells, but immediately she set about doctoring them. Perhaps she placed them in hot or warm water adding salt or a copper coin: perhaps she cut or pummelled their stalks. She then put them with great care in the various vases at her disposal. Again nothing was off-hand; she placed every flower into place singly, and this was a lengthy task. But it worked, and the result would give her pleasure for several days. When Welby motored her out of London every now and again, he would stop the car while Aunt Jessie climbed into a hedge for some campion or 'birdspittle'.

Once, when motoring with Pedro from Biarritz to Pau, no doubt to buy some delicious crystallized fruits, she saw a clump of wild iris growing on a ledge down the cliff. Welby was off in pursuit, for there was nothing he would not do for his mistress. But suddenly he found that, without great danger, he could not get back to the face of the rock. 'Stay where you are, Welby! Don't move! Keep still, Welby!' Soon Aunt Jessie and Uncle Percy were lowering a rope they had found in the boot of the car. A tremendous tug-of-war: 'Pull hard, Chesshie! Pull harder!' Husband and wife, with eyes popping, made the supreme effort as Welby was hoisted to safety.

Aunt Jessie's innate simplicity made her a rewarding audience and gave added incentive for the telling of an anecdote or the giving of some small present. The litmus paper did not wear out: she would respond in just the way one had hoped she would. There was never anything blasé about her; she was a perennial 'Bisto kid'.

Yet Aunt Jessie also had an eye for quality in things of luxury. Her instinct always told her which was the best in furs and silks: she instinctively knew about good wines, and race horses. She recognized and appreciated the workmanship of a fine piece of embroidery, a watch, or the lath of a shoe; she admired the tooling of leather, or the workmanship of a gold purse. She favoured all things for their innate excellence.

Uncle Percy made a dramatic foil for my aunt, and it was

like watching a little comedy to see her overcoming his dislikes and prejudices. He must have known, when appearing through a blanket of smoke into her sitting room, that his wife had spent the afternoon blowing smoke rings. Pedro strongly objected to smoking which he considered unladylike and unsuitable for a diplomat's wife. But, by degrees, Aunt Jessie did not even have to pretend that she did not smoke like a bonfire, and Uncle Percy became resigned – for he gave in to all of her whims.

However, when Ronnie, a yapping little black Pomeranian, first joined Tiny, the Yorkshire terrier, on the Compayne Gardens scene, Uncle Percy determined to put his foot down. 'Noh, Chesshie, we are not gohing to have any more petts getting under our feet! Tiny is enough!' Aunt Jessie raised her brows and opened wider her triangular eyes. 'Orh, poor darling little Ronnie! He's such a clever little thing!'

'Noh, I will not have him in the house; you must gett wridd of him! He's a little yapper, and I can't pear yapping dogs, Chesshie!'

'Orh, Peth-er-orh, you couldn't turn the *pobrecito* out!'

Ronnie seemed to sense that he was doomed, and watched and followed Uncle Percy all day with large, wistful eyes. Then, to make the situation worse, Ronnie, perhaps out of nervous anxiety, made a mess on the carpet of Uncle Percy's study.

'Chesshie, I have told you to get wridd of Wronnie!'

At the thought of having to abandon her little darling, Aunt Jessie's cheeks went white under the rouge.

Then came the night of the burglary. In the depth of blackness Ronnie, lying at the foot of the large brass bed occupied by Uncle Percy and his wife, started to bark. Uncle Percy was awakened. 'Woof! Woof!' went Ronnie. 'Pee quiert, Wronnie!' 'Woof! Woof!' 'Pee quiert, Wronnie!' But Ronnie continued to bark. Aunt Jessie, refusing to open her eyes, called: 'What isst, Ronnie?' But the barking continued. Jessie sat up to see her husband leaving the bedroom with Ronnie running in front of him. Uncle Percy murmured: 'I'd better goh and have a look!' Quick as a flash Aunt Jessie in her nightgown, her face well basted in Paris oils, followed her husband.

38

As he rounded the stairs to come down into the hall, Uncle Percy caught sight of the burglars. All over the floor were sacks bulging with heavy silver candelabra, dish covers, epergnes, soup tureens, and the contents of the drawers of the dining-room sideboard.

But at the sight of this huge, dark man in pyjamas with the wild eyes and fierce moustache, with Aunt Jessie bringing up the rear, while the Pomeranian barked and snapped, the burglars were terrified. Abandoning their spoils they raced for the dining-room windows, down the iron steps of the verandah, and into the garden. Uncle Percy, Aunt Jessie and Ronnie followed in hot pursuit and gave the men a good run for it, though finally the intruders vaulted over the tall, brick garden wall.

From that night Ronnie's safety was assured. He became at once the ever-beloved of Uncle Percy, who, next day, motored down to Tessier's in Bond Street where he ordered a silver collar, hung with bells, for Ronnie, with a medal inscribed: 'To a very brave little dog.' Aunt Jessie's cup was filled. Perhaps no dog ever was more pampered than Ronnie. A special coat of tartan stuff was made for winter wear. My uncle even felt that he could not bear to see his little pet with wet feet, so he ordered rubber galoshes which, on a rainy day, he took delight in putting on Ronnie's paws. The dog, however, was not so happy about this latest attention, for it was only with difficulty that he could manoeuvre his hampered way through the mud.

5 High Life

Each visit to Aunt Jessie's brought a new set of surprises. Perhaps she was just back from Paris, and already, as we passed under the stained-glass windows on our way up to her bedroom, there stood a dozen pieces of incredibly heavy luggage still to be opened. How had it been possible to lift these gigantic trunks from the train on to a motor car, and thus far up these stairs? Her bedroom was almost impregnable with other vast, shiny, leather and steel-banded coffins which were now open to reveal layer on layer of new dresses. Overflowing the confines were evening gowns with cobweb-like embroidered tunics, gossamers printed with embossed velvet appliqué work, with shifts sprinkled with sequins eventually to be worn ('Orch, buttzer knoh, it's such a good way to ring the changes') over different coloured satin under-dresses. There were a number of black outfits, for Latin Americans take their mourning seriously.

None of these confections came from Doucet, Doeuillet, Drecoll, or others among the best firms in Paris. Maybe Aunt Jessie's dress allowance necessitated her keeping within restricted limits of expense; but it is also likely that she considered that, by clever ruses, she could always obtain 'as good or better' from some up-and-coming little Frenchwoman.

One huge, basket, labelled with the *cartouches* of the Mesdames Lespiaut, Place Vendôme, contained the all-the-year-round garden of artificial flowers – poppies, violets and dew-spangled, dark red roses – which were in themselves works of art. A large, flat case was layered with painted and spangled fans from Duvellroy. A gigantic iron box was entirely filled with her face creams, lotions, and every sort of beauty preparation to eradicate the harm done to her complexion by the Andean sun. There were square black trunks with gold hasps at the edges: these were specially designed to transplant the huge picture-hats for which she had such a passion. Instead of going to the great hat-makers of Paris she must have become the favourite client of a Madame Jandrot. This lady had access to all the latest modes, and no doubt Aunt Jessie enjoyed the feeling that she was making an economy by acquiring a dozen hats for the price of ten at Marie Alphonsine or Lentheric. Madame Jandrot's hats, in the fashion of the time, were gigantic cartwheels with tall crowns from which sprouted a firework display of osprey, birds of paradise, or huge, funereal ostrich plumes. For travelling, these wonderful creations were stabbed with long, spear-like hat pins on to the wire-mesh moulds which were attached to sides, bottom and top of the hat-trunk. In this manner each trunk arrived with six hats in perfect condition.

At a time when the fashion was for all the soft pale tints of the sweet pea, my aunt would adorn herself in the most brilliant colours. She could by no means be considered to dress in impeccable taste, but she was too bold and sweeping in her sartorial statements to come under the heading of *kitsch* or *courci*. Although her clothes were flamboyant she had flair: she wore her huge cavalier hats and boas with aplomb. She accepted with gusto even the most exaggerated novelties of fashion. Spit curls were in, so hers were larger and better-shaped and more Spanish than any. The harem or hobble skirt had made the slashed skirt necessary, so she showed off to full advantage her minute, plump feet in diamond-buckled-shoes with the ribbon-lacing to the knees of her lace stockings. Diamond heels were trendy, and the higher they were the better. This gave her the great opportunity to acquire stature; being petite, her heels became so tall that she had to regulate her lilting steps with care.

Every visitor from Latin America seemed to make Aunt Jessie's house into his home, or relied upon my aunt for entertainment, gaiety and help. Friends had the habit of dropping in at all times of day and evening. This pleased her. She was never inconvenienced, never complained about being tired or harassed by people; she gave her own warmth of welcome to each. A whole afternoon would be devoted to casual chatter in the drawing-room. The formal chairs would be filled with ladies in black satin (they were not necessarily in mourning, but found black becoming to the complexion) sitting with crossed legs in high-heeled, patent leather shoes. Goodwill and contentment seemed to emanate from all. Some complained a little wistfully of their battle against fat – but large boxes of chocolates and pink and white and pale green sugared sweets, or crystallized fruits, would be offered, and temptation was given into with much laughter.

Outside the immediate Suarez family circle, there were many whose names sounded with such familiarity. Gutierrez, Solares, Cuenca, Benavides, Emma Dessa – these names would roll off my aunt's tongue with splendid gusto, and each of them, I soon learned, belonged to an important separate entity.

Madame Anna Suarez Alberdi was Uncle Percy's sister. She was grey-haired and green-eyed, with a face that never stopped smiling at you; perhaps she took refuge behind this smile for the reason that she could speak but little English. She may have suffered from poor health, for she seemed to have little vitality, but this may have been as a result of bearing ten children. Her husband, Juan Alberdi, was an Argentinian by birth, his great-uncle, Juan Battista, having written the Constitution for the Argentine.

Beatrice Alberdi, the eldest daughter, was the greatest beauty – in a pigeony way – and she accepted the fact. Her hair was of the blackest silk and her eyes the biggest, deepest pools. Her porcelain-white complexion was treated with the utmost care and her make-up was masterly; with an artist's restraint she made use of powder and luminous rouges, and coloured her lips in the palest coral. In repose she wore an enigmatic smile like a Madonna by Luini with the lips slightly pursed; but, perhaps through a sense of self-preservation and in order not to acquire lines at the sides of her slightly aquiline nose, she would laugh with the mouth turning down at the corners. Beatrice wore her marcelle-waved hair flat like the coiffures in Grecian sculpture, but she lacked the Greek column neck and, in the fashion that was about to start, sat

42

rather hunched with head thrust forward. However, this gave her an opportunity to look up with her large prune eyes more full of commiseration than ever. Beatrice, at her English school, had played the role of Titania, and this had instilled in her ideas of going on the stage, but such a career was forbidden by her mother who had strict ideas about how well-brought-up South American girls should behave.

Anita Alberdi was the only thin one of the sisters, and everyone agreed that with her delicate features and bones she resembled Pavolva the dancer. Anita related how she would accompany our aunt of an evening when she took the dogs out for a walk. Aunt Jessie would emerge with her face thickly covered with a solid white cream, explaining that no one would notice this odd apparition in the dark, and that this was one of her ways of keeping her looks and remaining young.

Of the other Alberdi sisters, Tina was cushiony and cuddly, Emily biscuit-skinned, but Julie, Tecia and Maria Luisa have faded in the clouds of memory.

Madame Alberdi developed an almost passionate love for her sister-in-law, and would hardly allow her out of her sight. She would accompany my aunt on her shopping trips to Paris, and rely on my aunt's taste for all the hats she chose for her many daughters as well as for the wardrobe for herself. Then she built a large 'French-style' mansion directly opposite No. 74 Compayne Gardens in order to be able to walk across the road and sit by the hour in my aunt's drawing-room, smiling and nodding like a mandarin while her many daughters filled the ears and eyes.

Their brother Herman was gentle and nice and dull, of enormous stature with a trunk-like neck, a flat Greek nose, and curling, wiry lips; George, called Gee, was tall and conventionally good-looking.

Madame Alberdi died young, and Beatrice, in spite of the discrepancy in years, became almost like a sister to my aunt; they remained together through many adversities.

Beatrice's other great friend was her contemporary, Herminia Borrel Taijo, who married Nubar Gulbenkian and was of a Praxitilean beauty. Her profile was pure classicism:

the continuous flow from forehead to nose was accentuated by her lips which, as she talked, pouted. She held her head high and proud and wore her hair straight back from the centre parting. It was always a special occasion when Herminia arrived, though she was entirely unspoilt and unconscious of her outstanding nobility of appearance.

The habitués at No. 74 included Romulo Suarez, a son of Nicholas Suarez by one of his many wives, who was the proverbial little monkey: quick-moving, with heavy eyebrows, long legs and wrists, and natty clothes. Another cousin, Hugo Boger, had cedar-coloured highlights to his tightly-waving hair, and a vague, tired look in his surprisingly pale eyes.

I was completely mesmerized by the appearances of these so un-English-looking personalities. From the earliest age I was conscious of the effect of pale powder and paint on the quite dark complexions of some of the ladies, and henna had a peculiar effect when applied to the blackest silken hair. The men all seemed to have blue-shadowed complexions, with a curious reddish-mauve glow around their nostrils, which I was to notice as being quite a common sight in my later travels to Bolivia. Often their fleshy, voluptuous lips were pale and unusually dry.

Jessie's South American entourage was adept at picking up English slang and music hall jargon, and the habit was then caught by my aunt. She, too, would exclaim: 'You *are* got up smart!' or allude to 'the fellow', 'the chappie', and 'the blighter'. She would reiterate: '*Muy bien,* that's a bit of orl right,' and end a story by saying: ' 'Nuff said.' 'I don't think' at the end of a sentence meant the same as 'I don't believe what I have just said' or 'No such luck'. She was often exhorting her friends to 'buck up and get well,' or telling them to 'stop talking tommy rot.' These commands were projected with a relish and with a strong trilling of the R's.

To how great an extent Aunt Jessie's stories were impressionistic versions of the truth, it is difficult to assess. Certainly she was far too direct a character to be accused as a liar, but she, together with her younger sisters, enjoyed heightening a story for dramatic effect. Somehow they always managed to add an acre or two to the description of a garden, a century to the life of a house ('Oh, it's very old!'), or a few carats to a diamond. When, in awed confidential tones, any of them would say of some quite ordinary acquaintance: 'Oh, but he's very highly thought of! You watch him and mark my words: you'll soon see his name in the Honours List', we were never surprised if the man in question sank without trace. The three sisters had a natural gift for seeing their surroundings and friends as more imposing than others would. This optimistic, rose-coloured view of life somehow never resulted in disappointment or delusion when their swans turned into geese; but it taught the younger ones of the family to take a great deal that we heard with a pinch of salt, and a lot of Aunt Jessie's accounts with even 'a peck of red pepper'.

At the time that 'Tango Teas' had become the rage, Aunt Jessie decided that she must take lessons in ballroom dancing. A small, bald man with spats arrived regularly at Compayne Gardens, not only to teach the Argentine tango, but also the two-step, the turkey-trot and the Brazilian maxixe. Of course my aunt was joined by several of the Alberdi family from the grey stone palace opposite. The beautiful Beatrice, in black, and other sisters likewise dressed, would place their arms delicately on their partners' shoulders and go through the paces on the drawing room carpet to the rasping strain of the gramophone. 'Walk – one, two, three – kick – one, two – twist and turn.' But no one went into the dainty intricacies of the dance with more abandon than my aunt, who would gyrate with raised little fingers and pointed, minute chubby toes. Then, through sheer exhaustion, but with roars of laughter, she would break away from some dark-skinned nephew and with a very small handkerchief mop the symetrically-curled fringe on her forehead.

'Have you heard Aunt Jessie has decided to have a French dressmaker live in the house?'

A spare room was soon covered with gauzy stuffs, chiffons, beaded and sequinned, and yards of swansdown or ostrich-feather trimming with which to edge a court train.

'Orh, buttzer knoh! This little woman makes all the

difference! She's a genius – every bit as good as Madame Subercajeau's Clarita!'

Aunt Jessie would leaf through a Paris fashion magazine – of great fascination to me – with the carefully shaded drawings coloured mostly in pale lemon and Parma violet.

'When she's copied this, then we're going to do that – not in forget-me-not blue, but in "tungoh"!'

Aunt Jessie attempted to furnish this spare room in the manner of a French dress shop, and she made a somewhat haphazard collection of picture postcards of current stage-favourites with which she decorated the top of a gilt and pleated silk screen. To me these photographs possessed the very essence of the theatre. An electric current ran through me at the mere sight of Iris Hoey, showing her gums as she smiled, holding a very stiff bunch of artificial irises; I was abject in admiration of the opulent Marie Blanche with rabbit's nostrils and cart-rut-undulating hair, while the latest smiling postcards of my favourite Lily Elsie gave me the terrible desire for ownership which only a collector knows.

But probably even more fascinating to me, because they were 'real', were the large photographs, mounted on heavy cardboard, of my aunt herself. Below each picture was the authoritative copperplate stamp of Lafayette or Foulsham & Banfield, Bond Street. Aunt Jessie had an ingenious, childlike enjoyment of being photographed; the results she showed with an enthusiasm she knew all others would share. As a young Victorian girl she had not acquired her later habitual look of wistfulness with raised eyebrows, and in photographs she appeared uncharacteristically solemn. Those that were taken early in her marriage – after she had achieved a certain maturity – showed her looking quizzingly above the camera with that expression of doubt, mystery and amusement, partly, perhaps, created by the slightly upward fullness under the eyes. In one pose, where this look was most emphasized, she wore a constellation of diamond stars in her softly-waved hair. Later she was seen in her most dazzling displays of paradise feathers, furs, and cinnamon coloured diamonds set in art nouveau settings. In some photographs her 1912 waved hair was triple-banded in the Greek style. In the more recent ones she wore spit curls and a Spanish comb in a much too wooden hair-do.

Aunt Jessie, as the wife of the Bolivian Minister, was automatically invited into the world-at-large and to all large court functions; thus she had the opportunity of meeting the important people of Queen Victoria's and later King Edward's day. But she was not cultivated by London Society; she did not belong in that strictly conventional milieu, nor had she the time or inclination for it. She was busy enough entertaining those she must and should.

My brother and I particularly enjoyed watching the preparations on the lawn at the back of her house for another of Aunt Jessie's garden parties. An army of men arrived with the trestle tables, and cases of glasses for lemonade and champagne and ice creams. Then the huge structure of canvas and timber gradually took shape. Once, Reggie and I became favoured guests, for the hordes of South American children were not invited, and we were ashamed to see the darker-skinned faces looking down longingly from upper windows as my brother and I wondered among the grown-up guests. Some of these swarthy ladies would pinch my cheeks painfully and say, with an envious gurgle: 'They are exactly like ripe peaches (peahchahs), even with a little fur on them.'

The representatives of the Argentine, Chile, Colombia, Brazil, Paraguay, and Peru had all been invited; naturally all the Alberdis, the Cuencas, and the Aramayo families were arrayed in their finest. Aunt Jessie had written out her special list, and the names read like those in a Ronald Firbank novel:

Doña Candelaria Flores
Doña Delisia Roca y tia
Doña Daria Coral
Doña Filomena P. de Alonso
Sra Primitiva de Aldunati
Sra Peneranda
Doña Felicidad
Dr Felipe Arano
Coronel Gutierrez

Dr Julian Eladir Rios
Monsior Vacas
Mrs Stumpf
Benjamino Bravo

Of all these marvellous people I was particularly struck
by a freakishly stout woman who sat in the opaline glow of the
tent eating an ice cream. Her name was Madame Triana, she
was American, and she wore a Gainsborough hat the size of a
hip-bath, trimmed with ostrich feathers. I gazed at her with
astonishment: there was something unusually perfect about
her – her skin as smooth and white, and her hair as straight,
silken, and as white as the unicorn's. Her eyes were so glassily
pale, the mouth lop-sided and babylike, and her chins wobbly;
I could not stop staring as she relished the pink ice cream with
a diminutive spoon. But what struck me most about her was the
combination of the two colours that she wore: I had never seen
pale grey and apricot in conjunction before, and the combination was something that I was to use a great number of times
in the future.

Like Madame Triana, all the ladies wore headgear of
preposterous proportions. Some of the crowns were like king-
sized kitchen utensils: salvers, tureens, moulds for Christmas
puddings or square cakes. Overflowing on to the huge brims
were the contents of a wheat field, the spoils from a rose garden
robbery, or windmills made of stiff ribbon. Every sort of
feather fluttered as they moved. If laws had been invented for
the preservation of wild birdlife an inspector would have
gained promotion for penalizing the wearers of osprey
aigrettes, birds of paradise, ostrich, gribe, heron, flamingo, and
even rarer unknown plumage. But no one wore a more striking display on her head than my aunt, who had selected one
of Madame Jandrot's most exaggerated concoctions from
among her latest arrivals from Paris.

On another 'occasion', given in honour of President
Montes, the afternoon was made even more remarkable for me
by the presence of performers, one of whom, a tenor in full
stage make-up and costume, sang 'Ciri-biri-bin'. But it was

the unbelievable prettiness of 'little June' (Tripp), a fifteen-year-old dancer, who later became known as June, then Lady Inverclyde, who made my heart flutter with first love. Astonishingly self-assured, 'little June' performed a slow motion homage, in a white tulle ballet skirt, to a large, artificial, pink rose placed on the close-cropped lawn.

Another special treat was to watch my aunt dressing to go to Court. Aunt Jessie seemed to be continually presenting more and more of her husband's compatriots at one of the Drawing Rooms which, at this time, were held in the mornings. In order to be at the Palace on time, the ritual started early with the hangman's call. In itself the *maquillage* – the application of many vari-coloured layers of creams, the fixing with powders, the blueing of the lids and the mascaraing of the lashes – was a lengthy work of miniature-like delicacy. The hairdressing necessitated an almost architectural foundation for the steady fixing of the Prince of Wales feathers and tiara; the corrugations of piled-up hair were as rigid as a helmet. Then, like a medieval warrior preparing for the jousts, she must be fixed into the inflexible harness of the long boned corset.

By ten o'clock the preparations were well advanced. We entered the crowded bedroom with awe, for this was a solemn occasion: we had to sit quietly in a corner as if in church. The bedroom was redolent with fumes of hot curling-tongs, the tang of singed hair, the metallic incense of sequin and metal embroidery, and the acrid calomine stench of the 'liquid white' with which Marthe was now liberally coating neck, back, arms and bosom.

For once no melodious laughter rang from Aunt Jessie's throat; the unaccustomed silence was broken only by Chilla, the marmoset, gibbering and shrieking as it scrambled up and down the lace curtains unmindful of the gravity of the situation. Aunt Jessie's three-cornered eyes had assumed a basilisk stare as she stood on a sheet laid over the crimson-purple carpet and watched the further adornment of herself – like an idol – in the many reflections of mirror. In the morning light from the large expanse of window the effect, with the magenta, Empire-style court dress and train, all intricately embroidered with minute beads, worn with gloves and lace stockings to match, the carmine lips and cheeks and ear lobes, was almost barbaric. The *parure* of black pearls and diamonds was fixed in place at throat and ears, bracelets were clamped like tourniquets on the upper arms and wrists, and a bulbous brooch fastened to the somewhat daring *décolletage*. Now Marthe was sewing firmly the magenta train of longer-than-regulation length onto the shoulders. The smallest Alberdi children gasped: 'Doesn't she look regal!' But to me this awe-inspiring spectacle of my aunt under the heavy panoply was the only time that I lost her.

6 First Stages

A love of the theatre, no doubt inherited from my father, was born in me at an early day. Before I was capable of taking in what was happening, my father accompained me to my first pantomine. At the end of the performance he asked me if the entertainment had been what I had expected: I shook my head in disappointment. 'What had you hoped to see?' my father asked. 'Elephants,' I exploded, dissolving into tears.

But having discovered, one early morning, when I was lying in my mother's bed as she drank her tea and opened her letters, a tinselled, hand-coloured picture postcard of *The Merry Widow*, I no longer dreamt of the theatre in terms of elephants. Lily Elsie was my sudden, irrevocable inspiration. Although the Rotary Photograph showed only the swanlike profile as it yearned towards some unknown romantic horizon, one knew everything about the sweet sadness, the compassion and the dignity of this glorious creature. This was beauty.

From that moment this four-year-old boy managed to discover other pictures and photographs and odd bits of information about *The Merry Widow*; the nursery gramophone wheezed out the 'Selection' until the record was worn thin. Lehar's music was so popular that even the visiting barrel-organ, cranked with a large handle, played its celebrated waltz until, suddenly, halfway through a phrase, it stopped; someone had opened a high window and thrown out a copper. The coin retrieved, the waltz continued – and so, too, my obsession with Lily Elsie.

My father was no doubt amused by such a premature interest in the theatre. It was something he felt sympathetic about, so taking another chance and hopeful that this time it was not too early in the day, he bought tickets for me to see *The Widow* at a matinée at Daly's. For several nights before, I had shown signs of being so over-stimulated at the forthcoming event that sleep was impossible. On the day of the great treat my father returned at lunchtime. He had bad news: Lily Elsie herself would not be playing the matinée. Would I like to wait, and go one evening to see the performance when my lady-love would be appearing? I remember the intensity with which I heard the bad news as I stared wildly out of the nursery window. My excitement was so pent up that it would brook no further delay.

Perhaps I had made the right decision, for it would not have mattered who was playing the leading role. I was too young to remember anything about the production except that a 'fast' lady had danced, kicking high her legs, on a table at Maxim's. For several evenings afterwards, in pyjamas and Jaeger dressing gown, I attempted the same outrageous behaviour on the wobbly nursery table; but I did not have the confidence of the dancer on the stage, and was hastily transplanted to bed.

The sequence of events is hazy in my mind, but I believe it was only a few months later that, wearing a pale blue silk suit, I was shovelling imitation snow with a mother-of-pearl and silver scoop. It was at the Carlton Hotel where, each winter, a children's party was held for The League of Mercy, a charity organization in which my aunt played an important role. The central hallway of the hotel, with its pretty tongue-coloured marble columns and gold decorations, was transformed for the occasion. The old-rose-coloured carpet had been completely covered with a taut, white canvas held in place by metal clamps and the whole sprinkled with iridescent snow. The shovel had been won by me in a raffle, and so absorbed was I with my present occupation that I paid scant attention to the fact that my Aunt Jessie was introducing me to a smiling lady in furs – who was none other than Lily Elsie. My Uncle Percy stood by. Forthwith I commissioned him to buy an enormous disc of Parma violets;. dutifully he obeyed. I then presented this very expensive tribute to the smiling lady in furs before proceeding with the fascinating job of snow-shovelling.

As I grew from infancy to childhood my love of Lily Elsie

ANG : Lᵗ Cᵉˡ Villalba Riquelme (*Espagne*) – Lᵗ Cᵉˡ Rodriguez (*Rép. Argentine*) – Cᵉˡ Kouzmine Koravaef (*Russie*)
ᵉz (*Mexique*) – Gᵃˡ de Hegermann-Lindencrone (*Danemark*) – LᵗCᵉˡ Ebener (*France*) – GᵃˡMᵒʳ Baron de Heusch (*Belgique*)
Cᵉˡ Suarez (*Bolivie*) – Cᵉˡ Jaccard (*Suisse*) – Cᵉˡ Chapperon (*Italie*) – Lᵗ Cᵉˡ Papadiamantopoulos (*Grèce*)
Lieutenant Colonel Jonkheer Van den Brandeler (*Pays-Bas*)

ANG ; Capⁿᵉ Bastos (*Portugal*) – Capⁿᵉ Blanco (*Espagne*) – Lᵗ Cᵉˡ Dragachevitch (*Serbie*) – Lᵗ Cᵉˡ Chéré (*France*)
Eshagüe y Santᵒyo (*Espagne*) – Capⁿᵉ Baignol (*France*) – Capⁿᵉ Pied (*France*) – Cᵗ Comte de Herberstein (*Aut.-Hongrie*)
Lᵗ Cᵉˡ Von Hugo (*Allemagne*) – Cᵉˡ Melley (*Suisse*) – Capⁿᵉ Didier (*France*)

ANG ; Chef d'Eᵗᵃ Lemant (*France*) – Capⁿᵉ Gay (*Espagne*) – Capⁿᵉ Mary (*France*) – Capⁿᵉ Micʼesco (*Roumanie*)
Comte Hishamatsu (*Japon*) – Capⁿᵉ Sjogreen (*Suède*) – Cᵉˡ Townshend (*Angleterre*) – Capⁿᵉ Lonkoff (*Bulgarie*)

A group of military attachés.
(Possibly photographed in Paris after a luncheon.)

Colonel Pedro Suarez, when Bolivian Minister in London.
(A carte de visite taken in 1912.)

After-luncheon coffee: Biarritz 1909.
Lily Elsie, Gertrude Glyn, Aunt Jessie and Uncle Percy.

My aunt's pets, Ronnie, Chilla and
Tiny, an essential part of my aunt's entourage at Compayne Gardens.

increased. Fuel was added to my flames of passion by Aunt Jessie's telling me that again, recently, she had met this lovely lady in Biarritz, to which resort my Uncle Percy and she were won't to repair for a few weeks each winter. During this last visit Lily Elsie, who was taking a holiday from *The Merry Widow* in company with a friend named Gertrude Glyn, had asked my aunt if she would chaperone them, take them under her wing, and protect them from the possible overtures of strangers. Together the four went for motor rides in the Pyrenees; they ate their meals at the same table in the hotel restaurant, and snapshots were taken while they sat smoking gold-tipped cigarettes and enjoying the after-luncheon coffee and sun on the hotel terrace. My aunt posed with her head cocked to one side displaying to its best advantage her tall D'Artagnan feathered hat, and there can be no doubt, looking at these groups today, that Aunt Jessie is the reigning star.

As a result of this holiday friendship my aunt had suggested that, when they all returned to London, Lily Elsie and her companion should come up to Compayne Gardens for a reunion luncheon party. The day was fixed well in advance.

I do not remember who were the other honoured guests, but a party of a dozen or more were sitting in Aunt Jessie's apple-green silk drawing room, chatting idly, sipping from tall, thin glasses, and smoking cigarettes as the two actresses were awaited. My brother Reggie and I were allowed to mingle with the company until the arrival of the celebrities when, immediately, we must disappear – to eat some doubtless delicious tit-bits off a tray. Then when the others were enjoying their coffee and brandy we were to be allowed into the dining-room.

By now it was well past the hour that the 'stage ladies' were expected; the large gold clock on the chimneypiece was ticking towards two o'clock. My aunt checked the time with her tubby, round, little gold and blue enamel brooch-watch. They were really very late! Had they forgotten? But actresses living in the West End could not be expected to realize how great a length of time it would take to drive to West Hampstead. There was no question of 'going in' before their arrival. More

C

sporadic conversation: another display of tall, thin glasses on a silver tray. Uncle Percy, who never showed any emotion whatsoever, sat with his legs wide apart and with his ringed fingers tapped his knees. 'There they are!' my brother shouted from his sentry post at the window. I watched through the heavy Nottingham lace curtains as Lily Elsie and Gertrude Glyn, both with bowed, but smiling, faces, hurried over the black and white marble squares and up the steps of the Swiss portico through the heavily panelled and thickly glazed glass front door. Quickly Reggie and I vanished.

Later, we were prompted that it was time for us to make our entrance into the dining-room. Arturo threw open the heavy mahogany door. A thick haze of cigarette smoke, spirals from cigars and the scent of melons and pineapples filled our nostrils, as Reggie and I embarked upon one of the most ill-rehearsed and embarrassing *divertissements* that has ever been devised. God alone knows where our appalling clothes came from, but I was disguised as The Merry Widow in a pale green nightgown that was so long that it prevented me from walking – let alone waltzing – and I was further encumbered with scarves and headdress. My smaller brother was an equally pathetic figure as Prince Danilo. I had discovered that the widow waltzed leaning backwards, with her hands placed behind her head, but I had not learnt, in such a position, how to keep my balance. Not only did we attempt to dance the whole routine, but we had to supply the music. Tum-ti-tum, ti-tum, ti-tum, ti-tum, tum, tum – (and repeat). To sing as well as dance was extremely difficult. Even at such a tender age I realized the performance was inept, shaming and abominable. It was as disturbing as the nightmare which has recurred throughout my life when I dream that I have been projected on to the stage to participate in some production before a hostile public without having had the opportunity to learn my lines. But in this instance the grown-ups provided the most rapturous audience; heads were thrown back in agonies of amusement. Even Uncle Percy grunted like a steam engine in trouble; my Aunt Jessie's peals of laughter rang through all the others and she wiped away tears of amusement that had fallen down her icing sugar cheeks. For this quite disgraceful piece of amateurism I was rewarded with a kiss from Lily Elsie. But for allowing us to be present on so great an occasion, I was always to be indebted to my aunt; she had given me a taste for the 'behind the scenes' of the real professional stage to me.

7 Summer Holidays

Every August my family migrated to the East coast in the belief that the rolling grey waves and the bracing winds of Norfolk would set us all up for the winter. Our tenancy of some small, rented house in Sheringham or Cromer had certain aspects which even I enjoyed. It encouraged me that I did commendably well in the local tennis competitions, and occasionally I had the satisfaction of hitting a golf ball bang in the middle of my 'driver'. The links smelt of thyme, and the woods at Pretty Corner were bracken-carpeted. Our nearest approach to a theatre was provided by a scarlet-clad pierrot troupe who performed in a tent, and the Lautrecian effect of the make-up in the acetylene lamplight was of endless fascination.

But these pleasures were nothing in comparison to the Kentish joys offered later in the summer when we were invited to stay at Folkstone with Aunt Jessie. No. 27 Grimston Avenue, her virginia-creeper-covered, terracotta brick house, was somewhat unsuitably named 'The Beni'. It had lots of white painted wooden balconies and bay windows, and showers of Dorothy Perkins ramblers. In comparison to the rough and ready everyday life to which we had become acclimatized, all here seemed so halcyon, gentle and highly sophisticated.

Nothing, it seemed, could ruffle Folkestone's warm sea waters. Certainly no storm clouds of approaching war crossed the Channel. Existence under Aunt Jessie's wing was a cloud cuckoo land. The household appeared to run itself without organization, arrangements were made spontaneously, and they seemed to work with this impromptu quality that had extra charm. There were no nursery rules, no early morning calls; the day started somewhat later than usual, and bedtime was protracted; one pleasure slid into another. No matter how many people arrived to stay unexpectedly there was space for them to sleep: extra cots were brought into a spare room, or a sofa in the library was used. The rambling house was always overflowing with guests. There were six of us Beatons, plus my sisters' nurse, apart from the many South American relations and friends.

During these holidays my aunt seldom bothered about dressing in style. Instead of her usual large hats, she wore a series of untrimmed straw shapes she had bought in Panama. She gave up wearing high heels in favour of ordinary cream-coloured gym shoes; these gave her a heavy, down-to-earth walk and a dumpy figure. She treated these weeks as a health and beauty cure. She explained she was giving her complexion a rest by wearing no make-up, and for much of the day she appeared with her face covered in cold cream. For hours she would play tennis wearing a long rubber corset, and we would laugh at her at the end of the session as, purple in the face and in a torrent of sweat, she retired to weigh herself on the elaborate contraption in her bathroom. 'Orh, go on!' she would admonish the scales in her deepest voice. 'Dash it all, I must have lost more than that!' Aunt Jessie's enjoyment of tennis was shared by all who played with, or even watched, her. Her performance was energetic and operatic. On her flat-soled feet she managed to rush after every ball, however difficult. Her service was extremely comic in its ugliness. She would stand to attention, then quickly lean forward with both arms straight behind her back; jerkily she would abruptly swing arms and body backward for a great overhead serve. Aunt Jessie's vocal accompaniments were part of the fun. She would coo, sing, yell, scream, or swear – but her language was never worse than 'Drat it!' 'Well, I'm blowed!' or 'Rotten cotton!' Her determination to win at all odds often caused her to pretend that her ball was inside the line when palpably it was out. When challenged she would say: 'Orh, tommy rott! Gett along with you!'

Often there were donkey races and bathing picnics on the

deserted sands at nearby Dymchurch. Sometimes the wind blew the sand into the sandwiches – and there was much amusement at having to undress and dress again with no privacy but the towel provided. The farcical appearance of Aunt Jessie, very tubby astride a small but fat donkey, being shaken like a jelly and coming in last in the race, was one of the super sights. 'Oh, buck up, Aunt Jessie!' everyone shouted. One afternoon the donkey-boy became exasperated with the laziness of Aunt Jessie's slow-coach and set about belabouring the animal to the usual no avail – until the race was over. Then the donkey took it into its head to gallop like the wind. With Aunt Jessie bent double as if riding in the Grand National, hanging on to her Panama hat with one hand, and the other clutching the reins for dear life, she sped along the sands at such velocity that soon she was nothing but a quickly diminishing speck in the far distance.

Best of all were the picnics and blackberrying expeditions to The Warren. This was a wild, mountainous piece of land with gorse and rugged chalk footpaths, full of tunnels and secret lanes. A somewhat mysterious aspect seemed to be inherent for it was so easy for one member of the party to be lost. Aunt Jessie, in musical tones, would call forlornly: 'Romulo? Romulo? Where are you?' Or, becoming slightly panicky: 'Anita – where have you got to? We're here. Whooee!'

One afternoon we set forth in great numbers, with cake-filled baskets and thermoses, in spite of a threatening sky. We scrambled up steep inclines in our gym shoes, and those in front were exclaiming about the magnitude of the black-berries they were already picking, when, suddenly, the thunderclouds collided with one another. The roar was terrible. Followed a dark deluge: the rain fell as if in the tropics. With-in minutes the chalk paths were a sticky, milky morass on which the gym shoes had no hold. First one foot slipped in the runnels, then another. 'Hold on to me! Whoa!' The gullies became streams with pebbles and boulders dislodged by the fast-moving waters and the rain was now pouring out of the black sky as if turned on full from a powerful bath shower. Everyone was long since soaked and Ronnie and Tiny were unrecognizable with their fur coats flattened to their shivering bodies. Soon laughter gave place to hysteria as, with a crash, one person after another fell full length. Progress up these steep ridges had been strenuous enough, but to jump down on to a glass surface was dangerous. 'Orch-to-taie!' came the Quechan cry. Aunt Jessie fell, unhurt, with her dogs clasped in her arms but with her gym shoes in the air. Somehow, with no broken limbs, but feeling that we had all been part of a great heroic adventure, we re-assembled complete in numbers. 'Anita, you're sopped!' The rain had transformed everyone's appearance. Hat-brims heavy with water had fallen over their wearers' faces; but the most fantastic sight of all was the Alberdi governess, Vi Huddard, whose purple and blue hat, trimmed with artificial cherries, plums and grapes, had melted so that the dye from hat and fruit had run down her face and neck, and coloured her dress in African stripes. A group of drowned rats piled in the motor one on top of the other, to be driven by the faithful Welby back to 'The Beni'. Then safely home, in turns we enjoyed the large, hot baths, change of clothes, and the laughter as we related the afternoon's experiences to the ever-serious Uncle Percy. His response was to suck air through his teeth and murmur: 'Aie, yaie, yaie!'

Laughter played an important part in this day-to-day existence. Generally it just happened that something spontaneous caused so much amusement, such as Romulo falling off a tricycle on the tennis court. Sky-larking gave way to 'bear-gardening'. Sometimes the fun would be planned in advance. Dressing-up was encouraged as holiday entertainment. 'Oh, look at Herman! He's got a motto – always merry and bright!' Gee, appearing in brilliantly whitened and mahogany-polished 'correspondent-shoes', would be called 'The Knut with a "K".' Aunt Jessie never dressed up 'comic': she was invariably 'pretty'. Transvesticism was assuredly a 'scream'. One afternoon Bea, Herminia, and another Bolivian girl, Rosa Harrison, appeared as very peculiar young men in starched collars and ties, sponge-bag trousers and apache caps. To my shame I see that I have written the caption 'Some Boys!' under these snapshots in my album.

Fancy dress inspired a great deal of amateur photography. In fact the concertina bellows of cameras were continually extended while some members of the party sat, in the fashion of the time, on the sill as smilingly she opened the latched window. My aunt posed on her way back from picking the Dorothy Perkins for the decoration of the house, with her head held at an angle and never full-facing the camera. The click of the lens gave rise to her intense amusement and a peal of musical laughter.

To crown a week of wonders and delights there was Saturday night at the theatre. The Sheringham pierrots, both in numbers and pictorial glory, seemed very small fry in comparison to the touring companies playing *The Arcadians* or *The King of Cadonia* at the Pleasure Gardens, with many wonderfully evocative changes of Royal-Academically-painted scenery, rainbow-coloured chorus girls and uniformed men.

On Sunday mornings an unexpected hush fell upon 'The Beni'. The accustomed laughter would be absent while the household hurried off to, or returned from, church. Aunt Jessie, like a peasant woman in shawl and black coat, had already been to early Mass, and was now putting on high heels and her Sunday best to go to the mid-morning service. Those who went to the various churches of different denominations afterwards met on the Leas in front of the Grand Hotel. Here was staged a seaside version of a Hyde Park display of fashion. Everyone seemed to be enjoying themselves; Tissot would have painted the bright, fluttering scene with the full gusto that it deserved. The Grand Hotel was undoubtedly the focal point of all this activity, and the shaven lawns in front of this vast, red-brick establishment were the most trodden upon. Ticket collectors punched the pale green and blue pieces of paper with a musical bell-chime for those who had successfully found themselves chairs from which to watch the passers-by on the asphalt paths. Loosely-uniformed attendants sold for twopence the programme of music being played in the elaborate pagoda by the military band. It read: –

The Folkstone Municipal Orchestra
(By permission of the Folkestone Corporation)

PROGRAMME

1	Allegretto from the Eighth Symphony	L. van Beethoven
2	'Fingal's Cave'	Felix Mendlessohn-Bartholdy
3	The Largo: New World Symphony	Dvorak
4	Overture to 'Zampa'	Hérold
5	'Light Cavalry' Overture	Suppé
6	'Le Ballet Égyptien'	Luigini
7	Gems from 'The Mousmée'	Messager
8	Selection 'H.M.S. Pinafore'	Sullivan
9	'In The Shadows'	Herman Finck
10	'The Whistler And His Dog'	Arthur Pryor

Late one Sunday morning, in fact only a little while after the gloved conductor had started taking his men through the 'Selection', a great flurry of excitement was apparent among the crowd, and all heads were raised towards the central balcony of the *piano nobile* at The Grand. Field glasses were lifted. Had Queen Alexandra suddenly decided to honour Folkestone with her presence? Was it the King? Or some member of the Royal Family? The word went round: 'Lily Elsie – Lily Elsie – it's Lily Elsie!' Could it be true that on that white balcony sat my heroine? Yes, the information spread. Lily Elsie, the original Merry Widow and The Dollar Princess, and now appearing in *The Count of Luxembourg,* had motored down from London with her friend and understudy, Gertie Glyn, and two unknown male escorts. Lily Elsie was always known to be tired; she must rest as much as possible – otherwise again that slip would be placed inside the programme: 'Owing to the indisposition of Miss Lily Elsie, her part at this performance will be taken by Miss Gertrude Glyn;' and the *Pelican* newspaper would once more rudely refer to her as 'the occasional actress'. Yes, it was Lily Elsie – fashionably late of course; but where better could she come to for a breath of sea air?

Of all those eyes that were peering, half-shut, into the

distance – the better to focus on those small figures – none
were more determined to catch every detail than mine. My
idol was behaving just as she should: smiling and turning her
head this way and that; divesting herself – oh, so gracefully –
of her sand-coloured motoring veils, though she settled to
survey the scene wearing her large, green motoring bonnet and
matching coat. She was most animated, and obviously enjoying herself: she threw her head back and laughed at some
quip from her escort as he lit her cigarette. Gertie Glyn,
similarly attired in motoring kit, was tactfully less animated,
and leant forwards towards the leading lady with a deferential
smile.

I overheard the muted conversation between my uncle
and aunt as to whether they should send a note up to the
musical-comedy star inviting her and her party to join them
for lunch at 'The Beni'. 'Oh, please do!' I urged with all my
strength. But the discussion became serious. 'She's tired – she
wants to rest. She might feel it was an imposition or an obliga-
tion.' My aunt whispered: 'Just send her our love,' and I
watched the huge, back-view figure of Uncle Percy, in his
tussore suit and trilby hat, as he went towards the lobby of the
hotel to write a note.

The band had finished 'The Whistler And His Dog',
gongs had sounded in minor hotels and boarding houses for
the traditional Sunday roast beef and Yorkshire pudding, and
the Suarez party had already left for the midday feast of highly
seasoned dishes. At length Lily Elsie and her group retired from
view.

8 *Bolivia II*

Apart from an occasional disparaging remark about the Kaiser, everyone appeared so good-humoured and well-intentioned that it seemed as if nothing could ever disrupt this happy life; the blue sky continued to be cloudless. We none of us realized that these were the last holidays at 'The Beni'. The First World War began. In the wholesale slaughter the youth of England was being squandered. My delightful cousin Claude, who had sung 'The Honeysuckle and the Bee' on the banks of the River Eden – who later became a fashion artist and tried to teach me to draw in the manner of Drian – was almost immediately killed. I was too young to realize the growing menace, except in terms of an abstract anxiety, or to understand that the world as we have enjoyed it had vanished forever.

Somehow Aunt Jessie seemed to retain her usual effervescence and gaiety so that no one would have guessed there was anything wrong in the background of life at Compayne Gardens. But, in spite of the inborn secrecy which prevented my mother from ever imparting any item of news that might be considered unfavourable to her family, one dreadful day it was whispered that there had been serious trouble within the Suarez family.

Uncle Percy had no doubt longed for a child to be born to his wife, but by misfortune Jessie had not supplied this need. During her second pregnancy something had seriously threatened her life, and after most of her insides were removed, she was never again able to bear children. However, when a married woman with whom my uncle had been having a secret affair gave birth to a daughter that undeniably bore resemblance to him, he was extremely proud. In fact, so proud that he decided to present the lady and her child to his sister, Anna Alberdi. The reception was frigid in the extreme, and Percy promised that the child should never be heard of again. An even worse situation soon presented itself. My aunt became extremely puzzled to notice that on her half-day out Ella Mutlaw, the head housemaid, went out of the house dressed in imitation of her mistress in large hats and furs. Eventually it was discovered that Ella was pregnant. Dr White was summoned; Ella died.

But other troubles burst like bombshells. Although Uncle Percy and Aunt Jessie had welcomed Nicholas Suarez's various sons and daughters to their house as if it were their own home, Uncle Nico had maintained a continual jealousy of my uncle and aunt. Once when the old man saw a photograph of Jessie in her court presentation clothes, he tore the picture in shreds. Now the trouble-loving Nico had, as Aunt Jessie euphemistically explained, 'done the dirty' on Uncle Percy. For a long while I did not understand what had happened. Eventually it transpired that Nicholas had long since entrusted his export-import business, the *Casa Suarez* in England, to my hot-blooded, but certainly completely honest uncle. He now had the idea that Pedro was misusing the family funds of which he had been appointed trustee by his late Uncle Francisco. Nicholas brought a law suit to prove his right to £16,269. Don Pedro was requested to resign his diplomatic immunity to appear in a London court. The case went against him. Eduardo Aramayo wrote that Pedro was treated by the judge with an irony to which a former minister of his standing should not have been exposed.

Running the Legation in London had been an expensive undertaking. Uncle Percy had been more than generous giving large sums to charity – the Ibero-American Society in particular, from which needy South Americans in London received assistance; altogether he had overspent. The war had by now reduced the property value of all large houses in England, and for a pittance both No. 74 Compayne Gardens and 'The Beni' in Folkstone were sold.

One of the Williamson nephews described the awful scene at Compayne Gardens when the packing reduced the house to chaos. The servants were one and all convulsed in tears.

In one large guest room my aunt exhorted all her nephews to help themselves. Piled high to the ceiling was the clothing from Morley and Co. which would not now be exported to Bolivia. In stacks, like skyscrapers, were hundreds of shirts, pyjamas and socks: shoes were piled in pyramids. The Williamson and Suarez boys, alike, ran amok. Ronnie yapped, Chilla hid in the pelmets, and Tango, in a large tin cage, was sent to me.

My uncle and aunt then left for Paris en route to Bolivia where an even worse reversal faced them. A rubber plant from the Beni had been smuggled into England where it was sent to Kew Gardens for inspection. It was soon realized that this plant would thrive in Malaya, which at that time belonged to England. Suddenly rubber entered the international market and the golden era of the Beni became sadly tarnished. In no time a new output of synthetic rubber brought an end to many a Suarez family fortune. Nicholas Suarez, with all his faults, was a man of courage and determination and, although no longer young, started a successful business of cattle-rearing and exploiting the tropical almond. Meanwhile, Pedro's friend, Ismael Montes, tried to have my uncle re-appointed as Minister Plenipotentiary in London, but the proposal was refused by the Foreign Office.

Nothing seemed to go right for my Uncle Percy and Aunt Jessie. They shared another tragedy when Ronnie, the brave little Pomeranian, was eaten by a wild dog.

At first my uncle and aunt lived in the fertile valley of Cochabamba where springtime exists all the year round. They had been lent a pretty house by an absent friend, and my uncle was given a remunerative job working for Bolivian Railways (a British company now expropriated). But soon Don Pedro was appointed Prefect of the Department of Chuquisaca where, according to the notes left by Eduardo Aramayo, 'his wife Leticia, in a very short time, won the affection of the inhabitants of the capital, Sucre.' Aunt Jessie, in her graceful rococo script, wrote home letters full of enthusiasm for her new house with its patio, tall, cool rooms, and the conveniently large kitchens; she was surrounded by so many friends. But Bolivia was once

more in the throes of revolution; innocent victims were torn
limb from limb and put to indescribable torture. Uncle Percy
always went to bed with a revolver under his pillow, and a
packed bag and his boots on the floor beside him; he never
knew when he might have to flee at a moment's notice.

I had little idea of what happened to Uncle Percy, but
he eventually returned to La Paz where he was acting as political intermediary in the division within the Republican Party
which came into power in 1920. At home vague rumours were
circulated that Uncle Percy was ruined, then had died of a
broken heart. We did not ask questions.

It must have been in the early 'twenties when we heard
that Aunt Jessie was coming back to live with us in the spare
room at 'Temple Court'.

9 Starting Again

We were all overjoyed at the prospect of seeing Aunt Jessie again, and the entire family had gone, in the greatest anticipation, to greet her at Victoria Station. But no Aunt Jessie; we returned despondent and worried. Then very early one morning a few days later, we were awakened by a pathetic, kitten-like wail from below. 'Hail-orh! Hail-orh! Hail-orh!' Half-a-dozen heads were put out of white bedroom windows. There below us in the rock garden was Aunt Jessie, trilling her arrival, wreathed in smiles and waving podgy hands. She was dressed in very odd, old-fashioned clothes: a huge, pre-war hat worn aslant, a pale cream alpaca suit, and cream calfskin boots with black patent heels and knobs of toes to them. Out on the street in Templewood Avenue was heaped a fantastic assortment of luggage and cages of pet animals.

In our pyjamas my brother and I rushed out to embrace her; the others assembled at the front door in their dressing gowns. Hugs, kisses, laughter. We looked at this comparative stranger with curiosity. How odd her colouring! How wrinkled her complexion under the pale mauve powder! How dark beet-root her hair, how sing-song her foreign voice! 'But come indoors, and someone will help with the luggage.' Did she realize that she would live off the contents of those trunks for the rest of her life?

Soon she was embarking on the story of Estrella, the successor to Ronnie – her faithful little dog with a black star on its face. Together they had been walking on the edge of the jungle when suddenly Estrella saw that a snake was about to spring at her mistress. With a leap Estrella was on top of the snake engaged in a death struggle. Within seconds Estrella's teeth had bitten into the snake's head, but not before the snake had poisoned the little dog who also now lay dead at her mistress's feet. 'Oh, I could never again have another little dog, and I couldn't stay out there without her! I loved Estrella too much!'

When she started to unpack she produced presents for us all: monkeys'-teeth bracelets, tomahawks, feathered headdresses, and for my cousins, Tecia and Tess, she had what appeared to be a collection of small shells interlocking around a flexible bone. Aunt Jessie related how she had come by it. One day in the Beni she was with a group of young girls who decided they would bathe naked in the river. Aunt Jessie was not feeling in her usual good health so she decided to keep watch lest some stranger should appear. While she was walking about in her long skirt in the undergrowth she heard a loud rattling noise. 'I turned round and there was this snake looking at me! "Get out, you blighter!" I shouted at it, and it shot past my skirt and settled down to go on rattling at me. I thought, "I'll have a whack at you!" But I couldn't find any straight stick anywhere, so I got hold of a very gnarled, crooked stump, and when the blighter came for my leg again I must have caught him – because he fell dead at my feet. I picked him up and went to the girls. "Oough, Leticia!" they all shouted, "that is a very dangerous snake!" You know I didn't realize it – but they said I'd been saved by my long skirts. Anyhow, we skinned him and here is the rattle.'

For some considerable time after Aunt Jessie's return to England her life in South America had more reality than the rather conventional one she was now living under her sister's shelter. Her mind seemed to dwell upon the early years of adventure when she first arrived in Bolivia. Doubtless she had recounted these strange stories many times to my parents, and since my brother and I were now at boarding school and were not often available to listen, she found my young sisters her most awe-inspired audience. In the somewhat deep whisper that people use when relating fairy stories she would re-enact the past.

'Orh, then Peth-er-orh, quick as a flash, brought out his revolver and fired into the darkness.'

'We were sitting in the patio after dinner, and when I gott

up to say good night – well, dash it! – I discovered an enormous snake had coiled itself for warmth in the train of my velvet dress! Orch-ta-taie! The other women all screamed!'

'And there was that time when we were spending the night by the Amazon and we saw a native girl, quite naked, lying asleep. To our horror we noticed that a large snake was feeding at one of the girl's nipples: her slightest movement might cause the snake to bite. So with great stealth we placed a bowl of milk on the ground as near as we dared. As luck would have it the snake preferred the cow's milk, and the girl escaped.'

Long past my sisters' bedtime the stories continued. 'Another night I was lying in my hammock covered with my mosquito net, and suddenly I saw two yellow eyes like balls of fire, and I could feel hot breath on my face. I realized it was a jaguar. But although I was terrified I could not move a muscle. I wanted to yell – I couldn't – until the animal moved on. Then I let fly. Peth-er-orh and the boys came running out, and went after it. And they tracked it down and shot it. Also they found its cubs; and I brought back the skins, and Tess, your cousin, has one of them as a rug.'

My young sisters eventually went up to the night nursery in such a state that they were not able to sleep for several hours, with the result that the nurse complained about the unsuitability of 'that there Madame Swaree's' repertoire of bedtime stories. But whether or not it was because my mother had remarked disparagingly: 'Oh, there's Aunt Jessie off on her stories again,' my brother and I, when we were home for the holidays, listened to the tales of danger and violence as if they were something that my aunt was making up as she went along. Sometimes we even felt like laughing with derision – as, for instance, when she confided: 'Of course I knew Colonel Fawcett, poor man! Peth-er-orh and I knew him very well. And one day after his disappearance I saw this tall white man in the jungle surrounded by Indians, and he gave me a sign of recognition.'

Why did we not believe her when she produced corroboration of her adventures? She even showed us arrows that had been shot at her and lodged in the thatched roof under which she sat while going down the Amazon in a canoe. 'The Indians on the banks were running after us and screaming as they peppered us with their poisoned arrows. Orch-ta-taie! We would have been killed for sure, but somehow our porters managed to capture a savage girl, and we kept her as hostage. When the savages decided to lett us alone, we set the girl free. Orh, I felt so sorry for her, poor thing! She was so ugly with a running nose, and she had such a high fever!' Yet, even if these accounts were accurate, they paled with repetition. The result was, Aunt Jessie must have felt herself unappreciated.

Another sad aspect of my aunt's present situation was that Uncle Percy had left her almost destitute. In fact, it soon transpired that my aunt's jewellery was now her only monetary asset. The collection was considerable. The diamond necklace, tiara and matching earrings were the most valuable, and there were two *parures* – one of black diamonds and pearls and another of black pearls and diamonds. My father, an exceptionally kind man, had a good legal mind. Much of his business took the form of arbitration, and I can imagine he dealt extremely fairly in looking after my aunt's interests. Uncle Nico was being vindictive enough to try and get his voracious fingers into my aunt's jewel casket, but this my father quite legally prevented.

Perhaps my superstitious mother was correct in considering that these black stones brought their owners bad luck, for certainly, when my father arranged for their sale, they were said to be no longer popular jewels, and the settings too ornate. However, they were converted into stocks and bonds, and with some large brooches and rings provided my aunt's sole nest egg. She managed to keep for herself some of her more modest and favourite pieces: a string of pearls, somewhat yellowy, with a handsome clip; several rings, a pair of hanging earrings of cinnamon diamonds, and a band of gold for the wrist with a solitaire diamond embedded in its centre. Also to follow her into old age was the plait of seed pearls from the end of which hung a heart of small diamonds. This had evidently been a fashionable piece, for my heroine, Lily Elsie, wore just such a necklace in photographs taken after her marriage to the wealthy Ian Bullough.

For the rest of her life my aunt could live at the rate of four hundred pounds a year. Although little in comparison to what she had been accustomed to spending, it was a sum which, at that time, was far from negligible, though with the years its value decreased.

Now that my aunt no longer had the immediate day-to-day activities of the Legation, and since many of her South American friends had dispersed through the effects of war, time at first may have hung rather heavily on her. My mother's tastes and way of life were quieter than her sister's. Welby was no longer at hand to drive my aunt about in a car with a basket-work body: there was no private sitting room where she could see her friends. But she never complained, or repined for her days of luxury; she was adept at making the best of things. She went into the kitchen – not to give an order, but to experiment with certain dishes. At some time in her life Aunt Jessie had befriended a wonderful old Indian cook named Isabel Villegas who, when almost reaching the age of ninety, came to work for us. It was not to be wondered at that Isabel eventually became too decrepit to turn out four meals a day for a large, hungry family. In Sucre Aunt Jessie had become interested in cooking and brought home many exotic recipes. She now took the opportunity of invading the kitchen to help out Isabel. Aunt Jessie's 'specialties' were received with raptures: her *arroz a la Valenciana* was one of our great standbys; her *empanadas,* made of chopped meat, eggs, olives, onions and raisins, or salmon, in pink-tinted pastry, were also our joy; and a wonderful dish of *chunos,* a dehydrated potato which had been squeezed or stamped upon to get rid of its juices, and then left out in the open to freeze in the very cold nights of the Andes: the taste is of *marrons.* Another favourite was a potato by-product called *tunta,* prepared by leaving it for several days in very cold running water in the open. *Membrillo* was a thick quince jam which cut like jelly.

One day, when returning home for luncheon from Harrow with some grand school friends, Aunt Jessie appeared triumphantly, with flushed face and dishevelled hair, saying that she had just cooked us a wonderful meal. With everlasting

remorse and miserable guilt I will always remember how snob-
bishly I felt ashamed of her. It *was* a wonderful meal to which
my friends and I tucked in with great gluttony, enjoying second
helpings of every course from the *empanadas* to the strange,
chalky cream, flavoured with an unknown pink fruit. But I was
at an age, and of a pretentiousness, when I would have preferred her to have kept secret the fact that she had in any way
participated in the preparation of the meal.

Yet in spite of setbacks, Aunt Jessie continued to be a
gala personality. Every day was a celebration for her: she was
always gay and ready for fun. A sport, she would drop anything
she might be doing to accept a spontaneous invitation. When,
a few years later, my extremely reckless young brother suggested taking her out for a spin in his new sports car, Aunt
Jessie immediately jumped at the offer. My brother drove as
if at Brooklands. Whereas spectators were utterly appalled as
they watched the car fly round corners on one wheel, Aunt
Jessie was thrilled. 'Ooh! Lovely that!' she said on her safe
arrival home. She could not see any danger in certain situations.

But Aunt Jessie was 'strong meat' for an everyday diet.
Although my brother, sisters and I were overjoyed by this
highly-coloured addition to the household, there were times
when my parents felt slightly overwhelmed. In earlier days
Aunt Jessie and my father had been great friends. They had
enjoyed much joking and horseplay; in a family album a snapshot showed my father holding my aunt's hand in a mock
love-scene on the terrace of the Monte Carlo Casino. But with
the years my father had become somewhat taciturn and
depressed. Perhaps already his timber business had started to
show the effects of war and its aftermath; cement was taking
the place of lumber in the newest building projects. Did he feel
his inability to communicate with his children, and that they
were showing an independence that he did not welcome?
Certainly his eldest son, who showed no particular ability in any
field, and was not by nature a sportsman, was a disappointment
to him. Whatever the reasons, my father became sad and
severe. He disapproved of any artifice to the extent that he

would not allow my mother to use make-up. Aunt Jessie was so heavily coated in powder, paint and pomatum that my father tried to avert his eyes, and to make things worse she was scented with all the blossoms of Arabia. Moreover, my aunt did not possess the gift of silence. I believe that she thought it would help the general situation if all the while she prattled and laughed and made sympathetic noises; so well-meaning was she, that she became indefatigable in this respect. But for my father to return home from the City tired each evening, and have to put up with his sister-in-law's onslaught of optimism and enthusiasm was the last thing that he had bargained for.

Perhaps he even dreaded the fact that his so very English family life was in danger of becoming South Americanized. Not only was an old Indian cook established in our kitchen so that my father complained of so much 'tampering' with chickens or beef, but a dark, wiry little orphan infant arrived: Carmen, the last-born of the large Alberdi clan, was being given a home upstairs on the nursery floor. Carmen was a strange child with protruding lower teeth, huge eyes and a deep, guttural voice. As a linguist she was very backward, and for a year the only word she could rasp out was 'gravy'.

My mother, wishing to do the right thing by both husband and sister, was placed in an awkward situation; she could not continue indefinitely to allow the worsening of relations. Sometimes my father's temper was really unpardonably bad, and Aunt Jessie must have resented his rudeness – except that she seldom resented anything. She had learnt not to be argumentative, so she shrugged her shoulders and said: 'Orh well! . . .' and went up to her bedroom.

But where could Aunt Jessie live?

My mother finally persuaded my father to sell the Hampstead house and come 'down town' to a smaller house. Whether or not the fact that my father was swayed in his decision to acquiesce, to live in the polluted air of Bayswater, had anything to do with Aunt Jessie's proximity I do not know, but all agreed she must now be on her own. But could she find some place to suit her temperament and taste, and her greatly reduced pocket?

Before any decision could be taken there was a reprieve. Immediately after moving into No. 3 Hyde Park Street my father went on a business trip to Mobile, Pensacola, New York and Ottawa. My mother accompanied him: my aunt was left to look after the children. No doubt we all felt a sudden sense of liberty, and enjoyed being outrageously spoilt; but the peace of the new abode was wrecked by Nurse Collard declaring war on 'that Madame Swaree – she should be sent into a bin!' She would *not* have the girls coming to bed frightened out of their wits by bloodcurdling stories!

My parents returned in time to put an end to hostilities, and my mother set about helping to find a new home for her sister.

10 Old Age

At this time, between the two wars, accepted social differences were still considered important. There was, among 'respectable people' in London, a very definite area in which it was 'possible' to live. Mayfair was the *comble* of elegance (though Shepherd's Market was shady), and Belgravia had its own magnificence; Kensington was definitely dowdy, and Regent's Park remote. Few fashionable people, with the exception of certain friends of the Prince of Wales, had the audacity to take up residences in St John's Wood or Paddington; but Aunt Jessie found herself a flat far away past 'that dreadful Edgware Road', in a neighbourhood where it was known that tarts lived, Maida Vale. Yet not for one moment did it cross my aunt's mind that she was not living at 'a good address'; such forms of snobbery simply had never existed for her. All that mattered was that she was surrounded by her remaining possessions, the household effects, which had recently arrived, though somewhat chipped and damaged, from Sucre. She rented a maisonette on the first floor of an ugly Victorian house with large, plate-glass windows, from a kind man and wife who lived on the ground floor. From the moving-in day, the De Perry-Caves showed an eagerness to help her in any emergency, and within no time became their new tenant's devoted slaves.

Today it is quite usual for middle-aged or elderly gentlefolk to find that they have 'come down in the world'. They complain that the tax man takes whatever is left of their diminished means, and that the pound sterling is not what it was; but there is comfort for them in that so many of their friends and contemporaries are suffering alike. They may even take a certain pride in being of the new poor.

It was harder for my aunt to find herself in straitened circumstances at a time when such occurrences were comparatively rare. Not for her the luxury of free dentures and wigs, nor could she claim the advantages of a state pension. Although no one ever had more loyal friends, especially among the Latin American colony in London, as often happens when money flies out, friends disappear. My aunt was scarcely aware of this, but it nevertheless annoyed her that one of her erstwhile habitués, having become Consul-General, should not have paid her a little more attention. She merely shrugged her shoulders and said: 'Orch! If he's too busy going high in the world, lett him gett on with it.' As for the more blatant fair-weather friends, she did not appear to notice that the sun had gone behind the grey clouds. Nevertheless, the first few months of winter alone in her flat must have marked the nadir in her life.

Her natural resilience soon came to her aid. She found everyone in the shops so attentive and kind: 'Nothing is too much trouble for them!' she would say. And of course she soon found a special little 'hat woman'. 'Oh, Modom, that's you!' the little 'find' would say – and for some time my family were disrespectful enough to refer to our cherished aunt as 'Modom'.

On festive occasions Aunt Jessie, in yellowing chinchilla, thinning caracul, sad sables, or other relics of former grandeur including, no doubt, a bird of paradise shooting straight up from an inadequate little hat, with her face painted many tones lighter than her neck, would stand in the drab climate of W.2 waiting for a No. 28 bus to take her to a family gathering. 'Orh, but I mean to say,' she confided on arrival, 'from where I live you're in no time in the West End.' In fact 'Modom' found great interest and amusement in her bus rides. In her most conspiratorial of voices she told my mother and sisters: 'Orh, buttzer knoh, I met such a charming woman in the bus.' 'There was such a well-dressed woman who got on at Marble Arch today.' I'm afraid 'Modom's' bus stories became as numerous as her old jungle tales. It was certainly a fact that when 'Modom' boarded any form of public transport she created quite a stir.

The conductor would make some complimentary remark, she would laugh good-humouredly, and her special quality cheered up everyone.

But the greatest advantage of her new home was the fact that nearby were the Catholic Church of Our Lady in Lisson Grove, and the Convent of the Sisters of Mercy. 'Oh, these little Sisters, they are so good to me!' But Aunt Jessie was good to them. She was such a devout Catholic that her religion had come to be the most important thing in her life. Although she spent her savings carefully she was always taking a wad of pound notes along to the priest. She could have afforded more luxuries for herself, but she was frightened lest there should not be enough for her in old age.

By degrees by aunt was able to call in a decorator, and she proudly invited me to come and see her newly painted kitchen.

'What colour is it?'

'Orh, tungoh, of course.'

Then the walls of the drawing room became a virulent yellow: on them were hung her collection of the Cuzco School of paintings. These were mostly eighteenth-century attempts by Indian painters to portray on wood, copper, tin or canvas specific biblical scenes according to the instructions of their Spanish masters. Often the subject matter is harrowing in the extreme: Christ is seen rising from the tomb while the blood which is still gushing from His wounds is watering a harvest of grapes which the grateful peasants are collecting in overflowing baskets. Holy martyrs are being subjected in a playful manner to the worst excesses of cruelty that bestial man can devise.

Often the brushwork of these paintings is dry and drab, the grey, murky effects only heightened by the use of scarlet or embellishments of gold-tooling which give them an icon-like effect; but, in general, the more naif the attempts, the more delightful the results. In the place of honour was a large altar piece, painted on canvas woven of llama's wool, of rows of bishops adoring the Madonna, fashionably dressed in an intricately patterned lace robe and Napoleonic hat, as she stands in a garden of roses like poached eggs.

Obviously Aunt Jessie made no attempt to achieve a homogeneous scheme, and if at that time any interior decorator existed, he would have thrown up his hands in horror. Yet, with the walls so profusely covered with Indian rugs, on which were the heavily carved gilt frames of mirror and paintings, with feathered Indian cloaks, china Easter eggs, her heavy English pieces of furniture laden with Potosi silver, and the sofas filled with brightly woven native cushions, the sitting room had an Aladdin's cave aura.

By this time I had come down from Cambridge and, not having found better things to do, was trying to embark upon a career as a photographer. To me the background of a photographic portrait, as it was called, could be as important, if not more so, than the sitter. Having exhausted the possibilities afforded by the rooms in my family's house in Bayswater, I found Aunt Jessie's exotic rugs and tapestries extremely useful as backgrounds, as were the Cuzco paintings which were large in scale and done in a matt paint so that there was no trouble about light reflections. In many a corner of her flat was there something of interest to me as a photographer searching for the unusual, and Aunt Jessie could be relied upon to give up her sitting room or possessions at any time for my still jejune experiments.

In the absence of other sitters she would pose for me wearing her customary expression of eyebrows raised in surprise. Patiently she would remain motionless for absurdly long stretches while I tried to get my lights in the most dramatic position, then obediently she would continue not even to breathe during the several seconds' time exposures. She was quite willing to wear an odd assortment of clothes I had found in her trunks, or filched from some amateur theatrical production at Cambridge. If I were to camouflage her in a mixture of day or evening, ancient or modern clothes, she would never demur, or fail to explode into a colatura aria of feminine enthusiasm when, eventually, shown the results of our collaboration.

Undeterred by the absence of a cook (Isabel the nonagenarian had died) she spent long, happy hours, with a cigarette hanging from her lips, in her kitchen. (Instead of the gold-tipped cigarettes she now chain-smoked from a packet of 'gaspers'.) She scorned wearing an apron and was seen, ecstatically happy, in a black dress covered with flour. The flour and the pastry became embedded in her diamond brooches and rings, and her pointed little fingernails would shred their layers of varnish into the toffee, peppermint creams, or the sweets of orange jelly. (These were 'a little bit of something new', and were made of carrot with only the grated rind of orange.) But 'Modom's' *pièce de résistance* were her Spanish dishes: the *almendres,* the round and flat little cookies concocted with almonds; the *cuñapesrs* of yucca flour with cheese; the *masaco* of ground banana and cheese (this a favourite for breakfast in the Beni); the *ciceron,* a fried pork served with a sweet sauce; the *manzar blanco,* made with milk and sugar; the *turrón* of almond paste and nougat; the stews of scarlet egg-plant explosively hot with red peppers and Peruvian powders.

Sometimes 'Modom's' activities in the kitchen did, in fact, become explosive. One morning, not able to understand why the oven was so slow, instead of putting paraffin in the stove she poured from a bottle of petrol. Not only were the tango coloured walls blackened, but the entire flat was in danger of being destroyed.

Once, when she had been lent a cottage with a village woman, Mrs Eagles, to do the cooking, 'Modom' asked me to stay. When we returned from long walks getting celandines, primroses and gowans from the woods, my aunt could not resist the temptation of going into the kitchen and helping the nice old body in the preparation of the forthcoming meal, and at the same time chattering on about her life. My attempts to write my diary were made difficult by 'Modom's' completely unselfconscious flow of conversation. 'I'm also a widow, of course. My life has changed a great deal since Colonel Suarez's death. No one had a better husband. He thought the world of me : he couldn't do enough for me. We always had a box at the opera. *Madame Butterfly* was my favourite of all. It's so sad. She's waiting for him, but he never comes back, and she kills herself. *Probrecitá*! The Colonel was such a splendid man: everyone admired him, and the King of Spain thought the world of him. You should have seen him on a horse! His back was as straight as a board, and you've no idea of the number of people who'd come up to me and say the Colonel was the best shot they'd ever seen! He could get his mark every time. Orh, buttzer knoh, that was a man!' Since I could hear no word from Mrs Eagles I imagine she felt somewhat out of her depth.

In February 1926, the two sisters, Jessie and Cada, set off for a winter holiday. Whereas 'Modom' had known the French Riviera in the time of her affluence, the fact that each franc must now be counted did not seem to mitigate her pleasure.

She started a notebook of her continental trip:

'The hotel bus met us at Mentone and drove us to the Beau Rivage Hotel where we occupied a lovely room (No. 51) overlooking the sea with balcony and lovely sunshine flooding in all day long. (Seventy francs each inclusive per day.) I loved the place.'

'Went by train to Ventimiglia, walked round small town, bought fruit and sat on huge stones on sea-front and ate it. Air and sun divine!'

'Went to Monte Carlo and bought two nice hats.'

'Went to Nice and found the shops lovely, full of nice fashions. The Galerie Lafayette is a fairly good shop full of nice things. Returned dead tired. The hotel is full of frumps, all aged. We knew Capt. and Mrs Cussack and Mr and Mrs Crampton: afterwards we knew Mr and Mrs Cradle. Played bridge with Mrs Smith Gomperley and daughter, Mrs Van Meenven and Mr Cradle. I won fourteen francs.'

'Went back to Nice for the two-hundred-franc deposit I had on a dress I ordered which never arrived.'

The two sisters then took Italy in their stride. Sightseeing and admiring the sculptures and paintings by 'the old artists' in Florence took the place of shopping. 'Modom' had found new cause for enthusiasm: she had discovered Italian art, and the works of Bernini, Caravaggio, Botticelli and Lorenzo Credi in particular. She wrote home of the 'prettiness' of the Titians.

'Modom' now decided she must become fluent in the Italian language. Within a month she had taught herself sufficiently to make herself understood, and even though a few words of Spanish crept into her vocabulary, she was completely at ease conversing with the new friends she found on trams, in the museums, and in the *pensione*.

On arrival in Rome strange pieces of guide-book information were assimilated. 'San Paulo, overlooking the Tiber, has a grand *quadri portico* and is decorated with mosaics from pictures by Agricolo and Consonni. Ten granite columns complete the decoration.' 'The amphitheatre was finished by Titus and opened to the public in 80 AD with performances that lasted a hundred days, during which five thousand animals were killed and Christians were devoured by wild animals.'

One morning the sisters were given the news that they could have an audience with the Pope. So great was Aunt Jessie's excitement that her notes were discontinued after these words: 'We immediately ran upstairs and put on black dresses and took our veils with us.'

One would have imagined that 'Modom' might have been erratic in her ways of spending money. But although she understood little of the transactions my father had made for her, and she was extremely generous by nature – arriving in midwinter, on tired and muddy feet, with white lilac, leafless, from Holland as a birthday offering – she was careful not to spend lavishly on herself. She counted her few remaining pounds prudently and with trepidation.

The ladies of the Beni had all the time in the world for playing bridge and my aunt had become quite adept. Now she took up the game again in Maida Vale, and there was never difficulty in making up a four. New arrivals – young Secretaries at the Consulate – found their way to her flat and enjoyed her friendly company. Of these Mamerto Urriolagoitia, one of the senior Secretaries, impressed me most by his manners, his deference to my aunt, his sense of polite amusement, and the way in which he implied that he took his career very seriously. Urrio, as he was known, had a slow smile and a fascinating mystery about the eyes – eyes that had a somewhat unseeing, slow regard – which all the dark and wide-eyed young ladies found irresistible. Even as a young man he had become almost totally bald, and strangely enough this gave him added distinction. I was intrigued to see that one of his thumbs was missing.

The flat soon acquired much of the gaiety of more opulent days with relays of South American relations arriving for long chats about nothing, and friends from the Bolivian Consulate bringing packets of rice or ahi-pepper sent through the diplomatic bag.

Soon Aunt Jessie's spare room was occupied by the thrush-eyed Beatrice Alberdi. Her mother had died, and her father's investments in the Tornquist Bank in Buenos Aires had proved worthless; she too was experiencing somewhat of a financial eclipse. But she now found the time to indulge her latent artistic streak by painting china, tinting photographs, and even decorating lampshades with grapes of barbola work and watercolour tendrils.

Beatrice shared 'Modom's' enthusiasm for beauty preparations. Now that 'Modom' could not go to Paris to buy 'Diamente' creams and powders, she concocted elaborate home-made substitutes. She drank the liquid left over from cooked vegetables, and praised the beneficence of goose's fat with which she anointed her face, rubbing it well into the pores. Instead of her wash-stand being massed with heavy, cut-glass stoppered bottles, it was now a litter of old, squeezed lemons which served as substitutes for some more sophisticated astringent; instead of the expensive china pots of face cream, she attempted to eradicate wrinkles by brewing concoctions of glycerine, cucumber, rose water and egg white. These she would not only dab on to her own face, but on to the cheeks of almost any relation or child who came to visit her. A cousin one day paid an unexpected, but abortive, visit, for Aunt Jessie and Beatrice were sitting side by side, unable to speak and determined not to laugh, with their faces stiff behind thick, white masks of Fullers' earth.

It is almost always sad to watch the ravages of old age on any person whose appearance one admired. But for a woman who has been beautiful in her youth to watch her own *dégrangolade* must be one of the most severe tests of fortitude. It is said that the approach to dessication is so slow that the pain is less acute, but the moment of realization cannot be avoided.

Aunt Jessie's particular looks were not made to last. It is in general the big-boned, horse-faced women who improve in appearance with the years: the small features are the first to disappear. We all become shorter-necked and hunched with age. My aunt had never had any height to spare, and as her girth increased her legs became bowed under the extra weight. She became a little, wrinkled tub of a woman. Some people, in an effort to be ostriches, will go to any lengths in camouflage. 'Modom' certainly put up a good fight. She never allowed any-one to see that her dark hair had turned to white. She knew her face had gone to glory, but to cover the crowsfeet and sag-ging sinews she used powder and paint more and more ex-uberantly. When the upper lip became a fraction longer and the rosebud thinner, the carmine lipstick was wielded with greater gusto. But not even Father Time could touch the perfection of her little nose.

She never really admitted to herself that the battle against age was a losing one, and again her strength of character came to her aid. She knew the only thing left for her to do was to chuckle. When she came out of a church in a Dolly Varden hat backed with old paradise feathers, her face behind a meat-safe of a veil, and the danger points at neck, elbows and hands well covered, she would laugh at the wedding photographer who took her picture. She was going to be the first to admit what a tragic farce the whole play-act was; and, of course, in the end she won. Her great warmth of humour, her sympathy for humanity, and her courage, increased with the dreadful years.

Another widow living in somewhat less straitened cir-cumstances, but nevertheless enjoying fewer comforts than when she was the wife of a Lord Mayor of an industrial Midlands town, became a neighbour in Maida Vale. Lady Brooks had for many years been a friend of my aunt in spite of the fact that she was as ardent a Christian Scientist as my aunt was a Catholic; their arguments were often violent. My Aunt Jessie had always, as we have told, extremely tiny feet which had been much admired, but since, with age, she had put on weight the little trotters had become inadequate to carry this extra burden. It was soon necessary for her to go to the Marylebone Clinic for electrical treatment and massage in order to make the joints more supple and to lift the less curved arches of the insteps. The improvement was considerable, but from now on, long walks were a thing of the past. When Lady Brooks came to tea and boasted of the fact that every morning she walked all the way to Selfridge's and back – a distance of several miles – a very long friendship came to a grinding halt.

In order to add a little lightness to a family evening, Aunt Jessie would very often be asked down from Maida Vale to dine with us in Hyde Park Street. But, after the first warm greetings, little effort was made to ensure her evening was a pleasant one. She would find that her attempts to tell her stories ('That reminds me of that night in Cochabamba when . . .') had been nipped in their tropical buds, and soon she would resign herself to sitting back in her black plush afternoon dress, with bits and pieces of diamond jewellery pinned indiscriminately around her front, and my sisters' dog on her lap. With raised eyebrows and enigmatic smile, she would listen to us children quarrelling with our parents or with one another.

We all felt a deep and loving affection for 'Modom', but perhaps now we were somewhat patronizing in our devotion. She acepted without any chagrin her new position, with my mother in dominance over her. Her courage and determination to be lively were never dampened. At the end of a long, but nevertheless early, evening (a game of bridge was a final recourse) Aunt Jessie would bestir herself, put on the old caracul coat, walk alone in the dark winter's night to the nearest 'Stop' sign, and so be taken by slow degrees back to her solitary flat.

Aunt Jessie in bottle-green serge with blue velvet hat and chinchilla.

My aunt as I remember her being dressed for Court in 1912.

Aunt Jessie's health, except for a deep chest cough (in no
was helped by her cigarette smoking), remained as unimpaired
as ever. Her doctor said there was no reason to suppose she
would not live to a hundred.

Of all the old friends who remained as steadfast as ever,
and whose love for Jessie was mutual, foremost was the delightful Mamita, Madame Aramayo. This elderly lady, now the
matriarch of a vast number of children and grandchildren,
would send my aunt the railway tickets to join her in her flat
in Paris, and thence to spend six weeks of the worst months
of winter with her in her large Basque villa, 'Häitsura', outside Biarritz. Aunt Jessie was invited 'to cheer up the old lady',
and this she did automatically. My aunt wrote home ecstatically about the welcome from the Aramayo daughters – all life-
long friends – and about Carlos who, in the tradition of his
father, had become Bolivian Minister in London. My aunt
described the motor drives in the sun, the mimosa and other
blossoming trees, the care and comfort with which the servants
pampered her, and how she was given a quart bottle of
champagne each day before lunch. Her appreciation of the
good things remained undiminished. She would stand transfixed while the sun was sinking into the sea. *'Que lindo!
Que hermoso!'* she would murmur at the date-box sunset,
without knowing she had done so. She was happy. Like Dryden
she would say: 'Tomorrow do thy worst, for I have lived
today.'

Aunt Jessie never forgot a birthday or family anniversary.
Punctually, a carefully considered present would arrive with
an accompanying letter in her florid handwriting. Her letters
were typical aunt's letters, and her greetings and good wishes,
and enjoinments to keep well and not become over-tired, were
deeply felt and sincere. Only occasionally her own personality
would emerge from the well-tried phrases. When she was
staying at 'Häitsura' one winter, she heard the news of the unexpected death of my brother Reggie. She wrote to commiser-
ate with me: 'I had to leave the others and come up to my
bedroom. I was quite dazed. I felt such a fool.' In November
1938, writing from the same refuge: 'My bronchitis got worse

D

here and I developed a terrible cough, but I am expecting a syrup from Paris tomorrow and hope it will do me good. I think the sea air was a little too strong for me. While in Paris on my way here, I was longing to go into Suzy's shop to see her hats, but dared not as I had no intention of giving four or five hundred a hat yet. But on my way home I'd love to go in and see *how much* they would charge for one I may like. What is the name of your *vendeuse*? Is it Maude?'

No doubt having diplomatic immunity for so many years gave my aunt a feeling of contempt for the rules and regulations set down by the Customs officials. Waving a gloved hand in the direction of 'Peth-er-orh', she had for years walked through all barriers with her chihuahua dog hidden in the inside pocket of her fur coat; the Minister would have to explain the reason for her having bought so many dresses, hats and skin preservatives. Later in life, when there was no Pedro to look after her, she would bluff her way through the law. Once a telephone call came through from Dover to my father: my Aunt Jessie had tried unsuccessfully to smuggle in a spring hat from Paris. She had even gone to the trouble of taking out its label and sewing in its place one from the London hat-maker, Aage Thaarup; but her stitching was carelessly done as the Customs official noticed, as well as the fact that the large straw hat presaged the season to come. The duty to be paid was fifteen pounds but, like most people returning from a shopping spree in Paris, my aunt had spent all her money. Yes, my father would be responsible for her; she thus escaped being taken to Dover prison, but she was later made to pay a fifteen pound fine. But even worse was the fact that this beautiful, blossom-laden hat was then stolen at the Customs – a loss she could not forget nor forgive.

In her tango-coloured kitchen, with a cigarette-end yellowing her upper lip, she continued to potter about by the hour. She never flinched at the thought of disembowelling a rabbit or putting her hand inside the shiny entrails of a chicken to bring out the giblets – dark red, light red and primrose. She was extremely economical, and saved every scrap and morsel until eventually good use would be made of it – probably in a *picante* concoction of peppers, red chillis and rice. Perhaps her greatest stroke of ingenuity was the use to which she put the wire moulds from her old hat boxes which she had carefully preserved all those years. The boxes themselves, now covered in rugs, were used for storing clothes; the mesh moulds which had been the means of protecting the hats in transit, were now pressed into service as sieves for straining her soups or sauces.

As the years progressed she had become totally resigned to the life she must now lead. Having dispensed, by her good nature, with any sense of style, she seemed to have achieved an even greater sense of the important values. Not a trace of bitterness was ever shown that her life was not what it had once been, and I would venture to guess that her existence was an exceptionally happy one. Her great quality was that of appreciation. She had the capacity to enjoy: simple or sophisticated things could give her equal pleasure.

Germany again contrived to bring the world to the verge of war; practice air-raid sirens were sounded throughout England and the civilian population was given gas-masks. The instructions were that, in order to become accustomed to wearing these claustrophobic contraptions, everyone should put them on for a time while continuing their everyday business. My cousin Tecia one morning knocked on our aunt's bedroom door in her flat. Only a foggy noise was heard in reply. Opening the door, she saw Aunt Jessie, naked but for a silk vest, but wearing her gas-mask. From behind the mask came a muffled, but running monologue: 'Orh, buttzer knoh, they tell us to wear this blithering thing when we're doing our daily chores, and here am I trying to get into my dashed stays, and it makes me very breathless.'

When, some time later, I had been sent to the Near and Far East, Aunt Jessie wrote to me a great deal. Some of her pathetically unimportant paragraphs were struck out by the censor for fear they might give information to the enemy. The following describes a dull, wintry patch in London: 'I returned with a cold, which am just struggling through, and to crown all I left my purse in a bus with three pounds and my little gold bag value of five pounds. I have been to the police station to declare the loss and its contents, so there is a *chance* I get it. (I don't think!)'

It was a source of worry to her that she could not take on hospital or canteen work and was too old to be of any active help in the war; she had to resign herself to knitting and cooking. As eggs, chickens and salmon became impossible ingredients for Aunt Jessie's *empanadas*, her powers of ingenuity reached new heights. Occasionally a rare find of tinned salmon was used to give a semblance of resemblance to those other pale pink puffs that had once melted in the mouth. An onion would be fried and cut into very small slithers, mixed with tomato and perhaps scrambled egg powder to make the filling for the pastry which she rolled on the marble of her wash-stand. The sheet of pastry had to be rolled every hour, then left flat to be kept cold on the marble. Once more the rolling pin: once more the cooling process. The Bolivian Consulate still managed to send her some aji-pepper so the little pies were extremely savoury.

One autumn weekend a friend invited her to stay, away from the bombing, in a small house situated on a large estate where great shoots were organized. In fact, during her walk on the outskirts of a wood with her friend's dog named Dash, gunfire was heard, indicating that a shoot was in progress at that very time. Suddenly her friend's dog rushed into the undergrowth. 'Dash! Come here!' called Aunt Jessie. After a few minutes Dash reappeared with a large pheasant fluttering in his mouth. 'Dash! Put that down! Down, Dash!' Aunt Jessie at once liberated the half-dying bird, wrung its neck, and hid the windfall inside her overcoat. 'Gett down, Dash! Gett away, Dash!' shouted Aunt as she hurried home. It was embarrassing that she should, of course, meet the 'guns' on her way. They could not but have noticed that it was peculiar that her dog should keep leaping up and barking at her extremely pregnant-looking figure. But Aunt Jessie proudly returned to London with her prize, plucked the bird herself, and invited a gathering of familiars to enjoy the unique treat.

Old Age

When the bombing of London became a nightly horror she came to shelter with my mother at Ashcombe, my small and remote house in the downs of Wiltshire. For months on end the two sisters saw no one but each other and the semi-invalid gardener, Dove. My aunt felt that the only drawback to such isolation was that petrol rationing prevented her from going to Mass on Sundays. She appreciated the lovely isolation of such a place. She marvelled at a shooting star, a fossil or a mushroom: like a child she brought home half-dead posies of wild flowers, and once she discovered a thunderbolt. She washed her face in rainwater, helped my mother with the housework, and made the best of the rations.

Yet, incredible as it may seem, even this isolated valley was not immune from the bombing. In the middle of a winter's night a German aircraft on its way back from its mission against Southampton, Bristol, or even Bath, had doubtless decided to jettison its one remaining bomb. It fell in the Ashcombe valley and destroyed the small cottage in which my landlord's gamekeeper and his family slept. Although shocked, they staggered, miraculously unhurt, up to the house in which my mother and aunt had been awakened by the blast, the shattering of the windows, and plaster falling from the ceiling above my aunt's bed. Even this emergency did not prevent my plaster-covered aunt from laughing at not being able to find, in the complete darkness, her way into a dressing gown. Then, having found her torch, she was chided by my mother: 'Put that out at once, Jessie! We don't want another bomb on top of us.'

In summer Ashcombe seemed to me the most halcyon of places. Nowhere else have I experienced more acutely the sense of peace that only sun and shadow brings: not one spear-shaped leaf of the ilex trees would tremble in the stillness of an ideal day. The cooing of the doves soothed one to drowsiness, and the sound of the hand pump drawing water would bring one back to the delightful realization of what the English countryside, at its best, can be.

But in winter Ashcombe seemed to attract the most violent of thunderstorms. Maybe the hills and valleys of the downs acted as a gigantic sound-box for these superb manifestations. At night the heavens would be fork-lit with blinding flashes, and then immediately it would seem that all the drums of the orchestra were rolling to split the ears. The rain sluiced down with such vehemence that soon the steep chalk path to the house would gurgle like a milky river. In the tornado the trees were bent beyond their endurance, and only later would we discover the broken limbs.

Meanwhile, the storm raged and my aunt would be outside with her head turned towards the rain.

'Jessie, come back indoors! You'll be soaked to the skin, or struck by lightning!' my mother would warn.

But doubtless her sister was remembering those other great storms in Bolivia, which she taught the little orphan, Carmen, never to be frightened of. 'Every aspect of nature is beautiful,' she said, and here was nature at its most grandiose.

Once, when my mother was staying in the country and knew that my aunt was alone in her London flat – Beatrice Alberdi having long since returned to South America – she prompted me to telephone to see if all was well. It was not; the voice that answered was little more than a kitten mew. I rushed round to find my aunt lying moaning in an agony of pain from which she had been suffering now for two days and sleepless nights.

Perhaps throughout her life my aunt had had bad luck with doctors and specialists. It now appeared that she had been to have her eyes tested, for her spectacles were possibly outdated, and might have been the cause of some headaches. The specialist had put some drops in her eyes which proceeded to harden the pupils and produce one of the worst pains that is possible to bear. When the pain first started she telephoned the specialist, somewhat tentatively, to ask if she could come and see him at once. He would call her as soon as he could give her an appointment. Meanwhile, alone and without help, she patiently submitted herself to the most excruciating torture. Inspired by my aunt's increasing moans, I gave the specialist what must have been one of the most peremptory telephone messages of his career. An old caracul coat was thrown over my aunt's nightgown; she put on slippers but no stockings.

Her groans and cries were terrible as we approached Harley Street in the taxi. On arrival at the imposing Georgian mansion, I told the attendant in a most assertive manner that this lady must be seen by Dr — immediately. The roomful of patients, waiting dejectedly for their own doom, were appalled to have to listen to the cries of this wretched victim. Perhaps it was more out of embarrassment than compassion that at long last the specialist summoned my aunt. An attendant had the decency to escort her. It seemed an eternity before she returned, by which time my mother had arrived by train from the country. The glaucoma had been somewhat relieved, and as the three of us left the building, my aunt's moans had been reduced to whimpers.

The incident brought me the terrible realization that, even when dealing with the highest echelons of the medical profession, the small, unimportant people who have no wish to be assertive, may have to bear untold and quite unnecessary suffering unless they become positively aggressive.

The arrival from the Midlands of my Aunt Cada, and her decision to live in London, was one of the greatest joys to Aunt Jessie, and made all the difference to her last years. She would never be lonely again, and eventually these two widowed sisters decided to share their homes. Jessie quit Maida Vale for the Regent's Canal.

When first my Aunt Jessie went to live with her sister Cada, she was delighted to find that again she had only a few steps to walk to church. Here she prayed with undiminished fervour but, after attending regularly for six months, she discovered that these services were, in fact, those of the Anglo-Catholic church. When she confessed her mistake to Father Bernard, her parish priest, he called her a heretic. 'But the services were in Latin! How could I tell the difference?' But forgiveness was a long way off.

Towards the end of the war, after a lull in the bombing of London, my eldest aunt came down the front steps of her flat to pay a customary visit in the neighbourhood. Suddenly she saw a large, pink object fly past her. Imagining it to be the tail end of a German plane that had been shot down, she exclaimed as she looked up to the sky with a blessing: 'Look – those fellows have got him!' Suddenly there was a tremendous explosion. The first doodlebug had arrived. But Aunt Jessie, undeterred, straightened her hat and went off to take her Red Riding Hood's basket of *empanadas* to the little Sisters at the Convent.

II Death

My lease at Ashcombe came to an end. My grief at having to leave, after fifteen happy years, such a hauntingly beautiful spot was mitigated by discovering that a small Charles II house nearby at Broadchalke was unexpectedly on the market. Often when motoring along the Chalke valley I had admired its ornate brick and stone façade, and suddenly it was mine. Aunt Jessie arrived with my mother to help the moving-in, and gave me a generous present of candidum lilies which grew on the terrace to be taller than she. Aunt Jessie admired my new house. I was pleased to think of her pottering about the garden when my work took me across the Atlantic. My mother was deeply devoted to her elder sister, and whenever possible heaped her with kindnesses. But, if given the chance, Aunt Jessie's exuberant spirits overflowed at the sight of a friend or a newcomer, and it was sometimes necessary to keep her in check. However, it was once the cause of a family squabble when I forbade my mother to silence her sister; I felt that my mother had become too bossy. These family tyrannies are tragic, but often irrevocable. One day, in my absence, Clarissa Churchill called in from her neighbouring cottage. Aunt Jessie, on coming downstairs, was motioned by my mother to stay away – which obediently she did. I was outraged when I heard this, but Clarissa said: 'Oh, that's quite natural behaviour between sisters.'

One afternoon, when my mother and I were out, David Herbert – a great friend and near contemporary of mine, who has that rare gift of bringing out the best in everybody – motored over from Wilton, where he lived in a baroque house in the park, to pay an unexpected visit. He found my Aunt Jessie alone: he was delighted. But no joy could have equalled

my Aunt Jessie's: she now had a rapt new audience. She told
David how she had been the first white woman to shoot
the rapids; how the Indian savages, naked and covered with oil
the easier to get through the undergrowth of the jungle, had
pierced the thatch of her canoe roof with poisoned arrows:
she told him about her escape from a herd of pigs. She talked
about the courts in Queen Victoria's day, and how much she
adored Queen Alexandra. David sat on the edge of his chair,
too engrossed to light his poised cigarette. Aunt Jessie took
full advantage of this rare opportunity; she did imitations, she
cooed and laughed. Then she ended her 'Jewel Song' and her
greatest aria by saying: 'You see, I've had a very fulfilled life:
perhaps poor Etty, my sister, has not. But I don't worry any
more; I keep my mouth shut, although I see everything that's
going on around me! I've done everything and seen everything; I've met the greatest in the land, and I've flirted with the
lot!'

One afternoon Juliet Duff, another great friend and country neighbour, motored over to tea with some London friends.
They wanted to indulge in a little theatre tattle. My Aunt
Jessie sat in the drawing room hopefully waiting to become
part of the party. But her conversational gambits were somewhat remote: even if she were able for a moment to hold the
floor with some little titbit about Tetrazzini or Queen Ena of
Spain, she soon found that the anecdotal morsel had been
swept away by more experienced birds of prey.

Aunt Jessie, long since accustomed to making herself useful, thereupon decided to take away the tea things. With her
bandy, fat little legs, and now slightly distorted feet, she staggered across my *Lady Windermere's Fan*-décor drawing room.
As she reached the stone steps into the pantry below, an ear-
drum-cracking crash was heard. Poor Aunt Jessie lay in a mess
of broken china, silver tray upside down, sugar and spoons,
scones, butter and honeycomb thrown widespread. Juliet made
an offhand remark of sympathy, but tried to continue with
the racy talk about Nöel or Binkie or the Lunts. For once my
sense of values did not play me false; the realization came to
me very strongly of how remarkable was this pathetic little

bundle in distress. Naturally my aunt made light of the fact that she had scalded herself; but I now had no heart left for my selfishly gabbling guests and was rid of them as soon as possible. My aunt, with a bandaged leg, was convulsed with amusement at the ridiculousness of the incident.

Aunt Jessie was happy pottering about the garden and watching the activities of the great variety of birds which seemed to find their way to her as soon as she appeared. Linnets, ring doves and young thrushes behaved with less than their customary shyness when she walked up and down the terrace. One particular robin amazed her by its self-assurance: knowing that my aunt was likely to have a crust of bread in her hand, it would follow at her heels. The wagtails caused her endless merriment, and the yellow chaffinches were her favourites. But it was when a starling decided to build a nest and produce its young in the drainpipe above her bedroom window that she became completely absorbed. She would listen to it chattering and imitating other birds, and watch for hours each flight as the most ugly of birds would dart backwards and forwards with another succulent worm for the gaping, ever-hungry mouths of the young family. Only when, at last, the fledglings had safely flown away, could she settle down to the knitting of another jumper.

It was hard that Aunt Jessie, so fond of animals, should have been, for so many years now, without her own pet. She had lived up to her decision, after Estrella had been killed by the snake ('*Orch, pobrecità!*') that she would never bring herself to possess another dog. So all her innate instincts were now lavished on my mother's Yorkshire terrier. Just as she had spoiled me as a child, she now did her best to spoil Suzie. Perhaps I am not sufficiently a lover of dogs to enjoy their proximity at meals, particularly if they interrupt the flow of conversation, and Suzie had been successfully trained to lie on a chair in the dining room, peacefully assuming sleep, while we were at table. But she now knew that if Aunt Jessie were present she would be likely to receive attention in the form of titbits; I asked my aunt not to feed the dog from her plate, but she could not resist the temptation. Two greasy little fingers once more lifted a sliver of chicken-fat to the dog's eagerly-opened jaw. Snap! It is to my great regret that at lunch one day I burst out in fury at her. Aunt Jessie appeared so hurt and surprised that I have never been able to forget the expression on her face, or to forgive myself for such a lapse.

Most Bolivian girls start taking two years off the date of their birth when they are eighteen; as the subtraction continues, it is impossible to discover the age of many South American women. Although she loved people to remember her birthday, and was like a seven-year-old opening the presents and greetings telegrams with such glee, Aunt Jessie was always slightly coquettish and evasive about her age until, suddenly, she was to celebrate her eightieth birthday; then, just as suddenly, as well she might, Aunt Jessie became proud of her four score. She was still extraordinarily healthy; she would say with great aplomb: 'I suppose I *am* old, but I just don't feel it!'

However, there could be no denying the fact that her chest cough was becoming serious. No doubt she should have long since given up cigarette smoking, and as the years passed she became more frail. 'I've failed a great deal this winter,' she once told me. 'Orh, I've lost a lot of strength!' I realized, even given her strong constitution, that time was running out; I must make some opportunity for her to expand on the subject of her early life.

'Dash it all, it's so silly, I lost all my diaries! I could have made a fortune with them – like Rosita Forbes. But one of the canoes overturned when we were going down a tributary of the Amazon, and all my trunks went into those rushing torrents. Of course there was no chance of ever finding them: they'd be churned up into pulp. It was terribly dangerous – what with the crocodiles and the piranahs which strip you to the bone in no time. Of course I minded less the loss of my luggage – it was those poor fellows who went overboard. Orch-ta-taie! They didn't stand a chance: the crocodiles just went snap – snap – snap!'

In these late years her religion became ever more import-

ant to her. She developed almost an obsession for Father
Bernard. She would quote him repeatedly. When there was a
particularly black fog she announced: 'And Father Bernard
predicted it to the hour!' But I fear Father Bernard did not
repay her devotion with gratitude. When she visited him with
her purse full of savings, he was not impressed by the widow's
mite. When she confessed that she had caught a cold and was
too ill to get out of bed and go to Mass, he refused to give
her a dispensation.

Perhaps a rather surprising quality was my Aunt's practic-
ality and neatness. One might have expected her to be slightly
slipshod, untidy and careless. Not a bit of it, as she would say.
She was, in all things, just as methodical as one would expect
from the neatness of her kitchen. So it was with the arrangements that she had made apropos her death. She put by, in
notes, three hundred pounds for her burial; she made provision
for a very careful disposal of the rest of her money and possessions. Every little gift was carefully thought out: brooches to
my mother, the seed pearl plait to her other sister, Cada, other
bits of jewellery to be divided between my sisters and cousins,
a hundred pounds to the orphan Carmen, and gifts for close
friends. The Sisters of Mercy were not forgotten, and her
School of Cuzco paintings were left to Father Bernard for his
church; but I fear he appreciated neither the thought, their
intrinsic aesthetic qualities, nor their future worth.

Aunt Jessie's wide experience had given her a certain
philosophical attitude. Her assessments were always logical
logic: in many ways she was wise. She had a clear mind, an
excellent memory and a remarkable capacity for learning new
things; it is therefore all the more sad that she had not assimilated much in the way of education. But she had never been
trained to register facts, and of literature she knew almost nothing at all. She was unable to discuss history, art, European
politics, or the ordinary topics of the day. She would read a
book or a newspaper whispering to herself word by word, as
she progressed perseveringly across the lines like a child.

I myself have always regretted the limitations of my own
education, but without a common bond of interests, talk, after

a while, becomes stilted. I found it difficult, in her old age, to bring out the conversational best in my aunt. I would be apt to sit in silence while she talked on in a rambling fashion. If my mother were present, Aunt Jessie appeared constrained, unable to be her usual communicative self. I noticed my mother often conspired to prevent her sister from being alone with me. When my mother said good night, Aunt Jessie would immediately wrap up her knitting and obediently follow suit.

Either I had not the knack of bringing her out, or she had become so seasoned to my being a silent audience that when I asked her specific questions she became self-conscious. However, once or twice she would expatiate on her experiences, but she did so in such an erratic manner that it was difficult for me to follow. I would have to interrupt: 'Where are we? In La Paz or Buenos Aires?' 'Why was Uncle Nico so vindictive?' 'How have we got to Lima?' 'Who went off in a huff? Uncle Percy or the tiger?' After a while exasperation showed itself in my voice.

In spite of this abyss, this failure of communication, Aunt Jessie continued to emanate a warmer atmosphere of love and friendship than almost any human being I have known. This sentiment increased in depth the longer she lived. Even if I were unable to relate fully to her, my admiration and regard for her became greater as certain of my own values changed: I understood a little more the importance of the things she held dear to her. How sad it is that we are apt to appreciate certain things too late, then belatedly realize the quality of an experience or a human being as if they had had to grow in us before their full import could be felt.

The first sign of my aunt's final illness came only a short while before disaster struck. A firework rocket roars through the air, then as soon as it begins to wobble, one knows it will only be a fraction of a second before it falls in fragments to the earth. So it was with Aunt Jessie: once her usual robust health started to weaken, the decline was spectacular.

While I was abroad one August, she, staying at my house in Broadchalke, complained to my mother of her teeth aching. She must go to a dentist and have the poisoned teeth out; but she delayed. Meanwhile, her wrist became painful. Perhaps she had strained it when turning the handle of the patent washing machine? But no – when she went to the doctor he told her he considered the poison from her teeth had collected in her wrist; when she was feeling a little better she must have the teeth removed. But she did not feel any better.

On my return I went to see her in her London flat. She was sitting on a sofa by the fire wearing bedroom slippers and her arm was bandaged. She appeared very run down and drawn: she begged me not to look at her. Nevertheless, I noticed that her pearly teeth which, by being slightly asymmetrical had always added such character, had disappeared. I asked her why she was not wearing the teeth that the dentist had provided. She said her entire jaw hurt so much she could not bear to put them in her mouth. She complained that she had always been so healthy and strong, and it was hard for her to suffer now.

When, a few weeks later, she returned to the dentist to know why the jaw was giving her such unendurable pain, Dr Tuck extricated a horrible growth which had suddenly appeared, and sent it off for analysis. After several days of anxiety the answer came back that it was not malignant. But, meanwhile, the jaw was still oozing blood and pus, and the old lady was in an acute condition of discomfort. As the days progressed her condition became worse. Other doctors were summoned: she was taken off to Hope House Convent and placed in a very small room where every three hours for nearly a week she was injected with penicillin. But this rigorous treatment made her terribly depressed; her nerves were completely upset, and she broke down and wept like a child. She begged to be taken back to her own bedroom. Mercifully the doctor allowed this. But he admitted regretfully that the poison had not been dispersed, as was hoped, by the penicillin. A conference of three specialists was convened.

I had just arrived at Broadchalke from London one cold winter's noon when Maud, my secretary, telephoned. I was looking out of the window across the paddock, past the line of ashtrees, towards the distant cottages where behind them, the wood curves to the downs, while I listened to the news that the doctors had discovered that the growth in the jaw was a cancerous tumour. There was nothing to be done; an operation would be fatal, and there was no other way of treating her. The only thing to pray for was that the end might come quickly.

It did not: the next weeks were without end. The wretched woman suffered bouts of such excruciating pain that my mother nearly collapsed at the sight of her sister moaning and twisting in her purgatory. When I went to see her, she could hardly speak, having just come through a term of torture. Her face was swollen out of all recognition and her beautiful little nose pushed to one side. Yet she remained alert and interested in every symptom of her illness which the doctor had told her was 'deep neuralgia'. She was fighting to recover with tremendous will-power. Later she said: 'If only I could get rid of these terrible pains, then I'd start to buck up! Buttzer knoh, they give me such gyp, and when they come on I knoh they are going to last an hour – and somehow I don't feel my mouth will ever get right.'

Aunt Jessie had become shrunken – her voice frail. She could not open her eyes to look at me, and I am glad that she did not, for I was so anguished to see her in this condition that I could not hold back a stream of tears. She described how the pains that now were eating their way under her heart were so terrible that those she had suffered a week ago were nothing in comparison. Mercifully I did not see her during one of these bouts, but my sister Baba described the spasms and twitches. Each week the situation deteriorated while those who loved her watched and could be of no help; it was an unendurable nightmare. In my warm, comfortable bed I woke up in the reaches of the night and imagined so vividly this poor creature going through these merciless torments that I could not go back to sleep. Each time I visited her, her condition had deteriorated. Two weeks ago, propped in her armchair, she had been able, with baby fingers, to put a little sponge cake into her tea and eat a crumb or two. Then she had collapsed, and had been taken to the bed from which she would never get up again.

My mother and Aunt Jessie (right) at the Ranelagh Club, 1925.

*A tea-party of diplomats' wives. Aunt Jessie (fifth from left)
with white ostrich-feather boa.*

*Christmas party at my family's house in Hyde Park Street,
in 1924: Aunt Jessie (far left) and (centre) Carmen Alberdi.*

The doctor said that, in spite of her age, she was able to put up a remarkable fight against this voracious disease because her body was still healthy, her system strong, and her heart in good condition. For these reasons she took so long to die. He compared her to a Rolls-Royce engine; only one thing was wrong, and if it had not been for this carcinoma of the bone, she could have gone on living until long after she was a hundred.

Quite unexpectedly she would rally for a day and talk quite lucidly about the past: the garden parties she had 'dared' to give at Compayne Gardens ('We had such good cakes from Buzzard's in Oxford Street, and others from Barbellion and Gunter's'), and the dresses she had bought from a little 'copyist' in Paris, and the hats from Madame Jandrot, and the mountains of luggage the porters had somehow managed to carry. She reminisced about the days at Ashcombe during the war when the bomb was jettisoned near the house so that the ceiling fell on top of her, and how amused she was when, in the dark, my mother was calling: 'Jessie, where is your door? – where is your door?' Then she apologized for being such a nuisance to everyone. She murmured: 'It can't be very pleasant to come up and see someone in bed grunting all the time.'

When the specialist again called to see her, he suggested that if she were taken off to a hospital to have ten or twelve radium treatments to shrink the swelling of her jaw, the pain would be lessened. The trips to the hospital were a big ordeal but, even so, Aunt Jessie would raise her head to look out of the ambulance window with great interest as the world sped by. 'Oh, but it's such a fine sunny day! And what a lot of spring flowers already on the barrows!'

It was a terrifying procedure for an elderly woman in such distress to be left alone in the X-Ray room for five long minutes while the machine made a deafening noise in her jaw. Yet all the doctors said she was exceptional – that they had never known such a wonderful patient for her age.

But the suffering became worse, and the trips to the hospital had to be cancelled. Mercifully the jaw reacted to the treatment, and the swelling shrank, and she was less uncomfort-

able. But the vile poisons were now eating up at a pace the
goodness of her whole body. Suddenly her head fell back on
the cushions and she went into a coma. The Irish Doctor
Murphy from the St John and Elizabeth Hospital was brought
in by an Irish nurse and announced that he did not think my
aunt could last more than a day. I cancelled my Christmas trip
to Wales.

Every member of the family had, by now, passed from
the terrible sorrow of knowing they were losing such a stalwart
member of the clan, to praying that Jessie might, as soon as
possible, be put out of her purgatory. Even now Aunt Jessie
was convinced that she would get better once the pains sub-
sided. My Aunt Cada went to visit Father Bernard to beg
him to come to see her sister, to say the rosary, and talk to her
with some words of comfort. Instead he telephoned to the
nurse who, while my aunt was unconscious, set up an altar with
candles opposite her bed. The door-bell rang and, holding
another candle, the nurse answered the summons of a young
priest sent as a substitute. The nurse genuflected and backed
her way in front of the priest, and as Aunt Jessie regained consciousness she heard the young man intoning the words of
Extreme Unction. For perhaps the first time in her life Aunt
Jessie was deeply terrified: for the first time doubt came into
her mind. In the greatest distress she called for her sisters and
sobbed to be left alone with them. Her tears could not be
checked: she heaved in paroxysms, not so much of physical,
but of mental pain. 'Cada, Etty, am I dying?' she cried. The
Irish Catholic doctor had told my mother that he would not
allow Aunt Jessie to suffer. We were heartened by the thought,
but Aunt Jessie, who now realized that she was dying, moaned:
'I cannot think what I can have done in my life to deserve such
punishment. If it is Jesus's wish that I should continue to suffer,
I will; but if it is God's will to take me now, I am ready.'

Doctor Murphy went away for his Christmas holiday; the
Irish night nurse decided quite suddenly early one morning
to give her notice and leave forthwith. There were dramas that
are too sad to relate – and still the invalid went on living.
My mother, who tended her sister so sympathetically and

lovingly, described Aunt Jessie, with her head lying sideways on the pillow, as looking like a wounded bird.

Doctor Murphy, bronzed on his return from his holiday, was amazed at the resistance of 'this wonderful old woman'. My mother, quite desperate, asked if he could not give her relief from pain? Instead he prescribed something to give her more strength. My mother and I exchanged glances. Strength for further suffering? Why could he not alleviate, if not hasten the inevitable end? One puts a dog one is fond of out of its misery: why try to preserve a beloved human being in this terrible state? During the war in the Middle East, I had seen young men dying in the desert hospitals, but this was my first experience of witnessing an intimate friend or relation dying by degrees. That old people without any possible hope of survival are kept alive merely to endure more punishment, seemed to me a medieval barbarism. I had not realized that the end for so many people was not just a question of fading away peacefully, but a case of protracted, appalling, and quite unnecessary agony. If I had known what pills to give my aunt to shorten her misery, I would certainly have given them. I felt cowardly that I did nothing to help her.

The Christmas Day luncheon at Aunt Jessie's flat was a tragic festivity. Father Bernard had deeply disappointed my aunt. He sent her no message. Aunt Cada and my mother, who had spent several nights on an improvised bed, and I, tried to swallow the traditional turkey and plum pudding. Aunt Jessie had braced herself to drink a glass of champagne with me. Earlier in her illness, when she knew I had sent her a case of wine, she had said: 'I shall have a glass of that champagne!' Now, although she was so weak, she pulled herself up on the pillows to make the effort. The wine tasted good to her, and she had always been someone who appreciated the best quality. 'That was delicious,' she kept repeating. 'That was good wine,' she panted. 'Yes, I think I'll have a little more.' Then she toasted me and said: 'You can never be repaid for all you've done.' She went on to say: 'We can't do without you, Cecil,' and made a grand gesture of salute with her pathetically shrunken hand. I blew her a kiss: she blew me a kiss, and I left the bedroom.

After our travesty-celebration I went back to have a last glimpse of my aunt in her small lair with the religious paintings, the Spanish gilt, the Indian rugs, and the other relics from the squirrel's hoard of a long lifetime. She was in a deep sleep, but an unhappy, distressed sleep, for she was moaning. She appeared now like a little old cottage woman with a swollen, distorted face, while above, on the wall, hung a huge coloured photograph of herself as she had been in the days of her beauty. A constellation of stars was in her waved hair, and there was a wonderful quizzical look in her triangular eyes.

It is perhaps as she was in her days of glory that I shall best remember her – with the huge osprey-trimmed hats, the high, boned collars, the beaded evening dresses, the atmosphere of laughter and gaiety around her. Even today the memory of the excitement she created causes my ageing heart to beat a little faster. But I shall not forget the marvel of how she faced the change in fortune that old age brought. This showed her true worth.

On the day of departure for America I went to that nice old-fashioned flower shop in North Audley Street with its white-painted, bogus Louis XV decorations. Here I bought my aunt a basket of dew-spangled violets and roses – the sort of thing that reminded me of the luxury of the florists of my youth. It pleased me that my mother, who does not generally encourage my extravagances, said that it was a lovely farewell present.

I had qualms of guilt at leaving my mother and Aunt Cada to shoulder the inevitable outcome of this ordeal when I sailed for New York that night.

12 Legacy

My sisters wrote to me in New York of Aunt Jessie's funeral and burial. She had died three days before her eighty-sixth birthday. The small church had been filled with friends, the little coffin had been draped with wonderful purple velvet, the flowers had defied wintertime, and Aunt Jessie would have been pleased that the Bolivian Ambassador was present. (Since the war, Bolivia and other South American countries had been promoted to Embassy rank in England.) It had all been very sad, and yet, where Aunt Jessie was concerned, there was always a laugh around the corner. She had long ago paid for her last resting place and had been to inspect it. Now it was discovered that her plot at Kensal Green was at the very knife-edge of the railway; in fact, for as long as railway trains exist, she will lie as close as possible to all the express trains rushing to Penrith and the North of England.

When eventually I returned from America, my aunt's remaining treasures – the Potosi silver, the gilded, heavily-carved mirrors, the rugs – had been distributed among various members of the family. I was very happy to have a quite delightful Cuzco painting, which my mother had alluded to as *The Black Madonna*, and which, for the reason that the Virgin's face appeared of quite deep, bluish-grey hue, she considered horrid and a conveyor of bad luck. When the picture returned from the cleaner and repairer, the Madonna was seen in her earlier pearly beauty. This black and gold painting, in its original frame, faces me as I lie in my Pelham Place bedroom – a reminder of someone whom I hold in even more affection now that she has gone irrevocably.

But the most personal legacy was my aunt's small ruled notebook of black imitation leather, with about a hundred pencil-written pages, dated 26 June 1890. The end-papers had been scrawled over with drawings of flowers and trees, simple mathematical sums, shopping lists and prices, and the names of all the people in various towns who had come to call upon her. Just deciperable, underneath, was the title of the book: *A Voyage to South America.*

Aunt Jessie had often told us how her journals had been lost; but this, the first of the series, and the only one to survive, gives an account of her initial journey from her village in Westmorland to Trinidad, the capital of El Beni. Page one is headed:

Travells

*I*t was on the 21st June 1890, a lovely summer's evening, when I left my home and native village, Temple Sowerby, where all is so dear to me. There the lanes are so lovely & green, with that delightful perfume that Spring alone can give; the hawthorn blooming pink & white, violets hiding their graceful heads, primrose & forgetmenots adorning the paths where'er you go. So it was when I left my delightful home for foreign countries.

Shall I ever forget the scene that is ever-present in my eyes? The "les Adieus" on the platform as the train took me away from the sides of those beloved ones weeping tears that only a parent can weep.

After waving them my last goodbye, and alone in the railway carriage, I gave vent to my feelings with oh! such a flood of tears. I wondered: shall I ever see them again? or be able to look into those dear eyes again?

With such thoughts I arrived at Penrith Station. I was met by Ella & Percy.* They, knowing exactly how I felt, entered a cab & drove to Lark Hall.

---

* Her elder sister, and her husband.

Legacy

Sunday June 2nd/90. We all (Frank,* Ella, Etty,† Percy, Baby,‡ and myself) drove to Pooley Bridge, by Lowther Park, saw such a pretty sight: the militia camping there & the church parade band was playing "John Peel". On entering Pooley met Mr and Mrs Wolfenden, lunched by invitation. Lunch fair, walked by the lake side to "Ewesmere". We drove back to Penrith, had a jolly champaine supper and Percy & I departed by midnight train (saloon car) for London.

From West-end Lane Station we walked to Fairhazel Gardens§ where we stayed until Wednesday June 25th, when we booked from Waterloo Station to Southampton. Here we stayed at the South W. Hotel, splendid accomadations, wrote home & went to the Theatre (Prince of Wales), took a box 2 guineas, & saw the "Gondoliers" D'Oyle Carts comp. very good indeed.

We sailed from Southampton (by the S.S. "Medway") miserable & wet, no friends, & very few passengers, only three worth noticing. Then came this awful sea sickness, ill three days. But as we passed the Azores the weather became beautiful & sea calm. On arrival in Barbados Tuesday July 7th Pedro engaged a carriage & we drove round the Town. The streets were very disgustingly dirty. The Suburbs lovely, quite rustic & wild; the trees in bloom, one bright scarlet. The natives, black, spoke English – women do most part of the work helping to build houses etc. The Island seems to be one immense sugar plantation.

Jamaica: Pretty fair town with an ugly race of natives; heavy forheads. flat nose & protruding mouths, colour black, copper, & greeny. Hard working women, men lazy.

As soon as we sailed sea became rough or rather what the sailors called "choppy". I was very sea-sick, in fact so were all on board – some even worse than others, & they remained so until arriving in Colon, July 15th, where we were saluted with such a downpour of rain as one never sees in Europe. The rain

* Frank Williamson.
† Esther, her younger sister.
‡ Her youngest sister Cada.
§ The house of Walter Beaton, father to Jessie's brother-in-law, Ernest.

*held us prisoners on board the steamer, but at last, after great
peals of thunder ended the storm, we entered Colon Street.
Oh, such a funny street made of wood planks, roughly put
together with the railway line in the centre! As soon as we
started driving we were jolted up and down, like cream in a
churn. I "held on" for dear life until we arrived at the
Panama Railway Station. Eventually the hour came for all to
"take their seats", in the first class saloon, (pullman cars), and
the train steered out slowly, allowing us plenty of time to
admire the scenery. Soon we were running above a most
awkward-looking river so that I shut my eyes expecting the
worst, especially when the train leant right over at very dangerous curves. & oh the motion! we were all "land-sick" with
severe head-aches. such a rickety old thing!*

*Then the landscape became nothing but a swamp – all
water and reeds, with only a few miserable looking people in
huts spotted here & there. I was not in the least surprised to
learn that each sleeper of the line cost a man's life; so many
died from fever, poor things!*

*Nearing Panama we saw the works & machinery left rust-
ing & spoiling in the water, & already so much work done. It
made one sad to look upon it.*

*Eventually, having stopped at 29 stations, we arrived at
Panama. Imagine the journey! After alighting from the dilapi-
dated old train we entered a cab & were driven to the "Grand
Central", the best Hotel, in a square facing the Cathedral.*

*We left Panama on the "Serena" with many passengers
from New York. Was introduced to the Bolivian Minister &
family, Sr Bordas & family, Secretary & friend. Also introduced
to the Chilean Minister and Family. They proved to be most
agreeable & lively – especially Srta de Margarita Elisia. Arrived
at Guayaquil: good sized town, Spanish spoken, very hot
climate, natives passable. Pedro bought me two horse rugs, 35
& 15 pesos.*

*At Tumbes we watched the natives cutting a whale &
taking it in loads to the boilers. What a sight & what a smell!
The size of the mouth alone was five yards in length, eighteen*

men were seated on the tongue, cutting & chopping away its jaw. An old native informed me that 17 barrels of oil would be got out of that tongue.

Of all the places we visited Payta takes the biscuit: there is not a blade of grass to be seen & only one tree. For miles around they do not know what rain is. They say the sand is full of rich seed but it will not produce without rain. Every drop of water has to be brought 20 miles on mule-back & a dollar is charged for each pitcher. The place is a bleak sandy mess, yet the most uncanny thing is that it has a railway station & a telephone. Here we took on board about 150 to 200 cattle.

Arriving at Eten, we were greeted by yells & screams from Indians who were about to embark tons of rice & Indian corn, or better said maize. Lanscape barren & not a green twig in sight, & so it will continue, I suppose, till we arrive near Lima.

Still the company on board surpasses our English strain (although a little disgusted with some). The evenings are spent pleasantly we sing, or dance (a little of both often) & instraments are not scarce, as there are mandolin, "gitarra", banjo, piano etc. Pedro brightens the aspect further with a little of those natural feelings he displays at intervals.

Eighteen passengers were hauled aboard on something that looked like half a barrel, which was lined with the English flag. Both fat & small they tripped into this picturesque seat, then waited for the hoist; it came with a shout & a jerk. Later came the bustle of preparing cabins, scarcely room & accommodations for so many. Till now my husband & I have had a double communicating Cabin, but at about ten o'clock at night we were quietly informed we must bundle our "goods & chattles" into one cabin. So with sad heart, but a merry face, we began to pile our things one upon another; to add to our discomfort, they have been loading the steamer with 3,000 sacks of sugar. The machinery for the loading is close to our cabin, so until the noise ceased at 5.30 a.m. I never closed my eyes.

All bustle & commotion when we arrived at Callao, & went ashore in a boat along side of Varas family. On entering the S.

American Station found many steamer friends all bound for Lima.

On arrival at Lima we all walked to the France Inglaterra in search of rooms. Streets were crowded, being Anniversary of the Independence. No room in first hotel nor second nor third, lastly we were very well accomodated at Maury Hotel, three familys, viz. the Bordas, Varas & ourselves – after procuring rooms, we all lunched together, then went out to watch a splendid procession in "full state", several regiments of soldiers, each headed by a band. Then came the Presedent, & representatives of the House all in evening dress & embroidered coats. The sight was a very gay one, & every woman & child wore new holiday attire, most extravagent style & bad taste especially for hats.

The morning following, notwithstanding our anxiety to start our sight-seeing early, it was late when having congregated in Mr & Mrs Varas drawing room, & discussed all our days arrangements, we separated each to go our own way. My husband & I went to the "Exposicion". The Presedent, a very serious old gent. evidently much esteemed, distributed prizes among 4,000 children. But the exhibition grounds were too crowded for enjoyment, so we went by train to see the "Alamada", a long well kept path railed in with statues each side.

Back at our Hotel we encountered a whole host of visitors, the ministers & gentry of the place, who came to see us off. All accompanied us to the station. On the whole we enjoyed ourselves (thanks to the Varas family) neither very extravagantly, nor otherwise.

We arrived at Pisco, where the famous wine is made. Only, this year the crops have been poor. At Quito we took on bales of cotton wool etc. etc. a very pretty place with two churches (a very holy class of people).

On the last day on board the "Serena" Captain Hullah and I made out a programme for a concert. Everybody did their best to entertain each other: a few comic characters went off splendidly, & all seemed to care for me. After the Concert we

*had champain & all parted with good wishes for the remaining
part of the journey.*

*Morning dawned; at 6 am we rose, packed & watched as
we arrived at Mollendo. Oh! what a rough sea! It was very
difficult to get from the ladder into the small boat alongside.
We had to wait our chance to jump. Pedro was left hanging
by one leg until a wave brought the boat up to him. And it was
just as bad at the landing stage of Mollendo. However we
alighted in one piece.*

The best hotel, *& were kindly* cheaply *treated, after storing our hand luggage in our rooms. I was very curious to see the
church, but alas! discovered it was a perfect ruin! In fact the
village itself was almost entirely destroyed by the Chilians,
during the four years war against the Peruvians.*

*It was the same at Mollendo Station when we started our
railway journey for Arequipa. Poor Peruvians! The Chilians
had blown it up with dynamite so that only the framework
remains. And the people are such a destitute looking race. They
have not yet recovered from the shock of war, and nothing but
poverty stares them in the face.*

*Soon after the train started its long run, a dreadful
spectical met our gaze; a cemmetary in the desert, where all
the Peruvians buried their dead after the Chilians did what
they could by the way of slaughter. Hundreds of poor souls all
lain side by side – with only a thin wooden cross placed at the
head of each grave to indicate which is which.*

*On we sped at the rate of 22 miles an hour, stopping at
about five stations, each one a worse picture of distress than
the other. All was sand & rock of a very barren aspect. It was
a relief to monotony when occasionally we got a glimpse of a
cultivated valley, growing fruits & vegetables. At last we left the
sandy deserts for high rocky mountains. The train ran along
the side of 60 or 80 feet precipices! The sudden curves & the
fall below, made one shiver as one looked out of the window.
At times it required all the steam of the engine possible to pull
us up the hills; and an added danger was the length of the
cars in which we travelled round the sharp curves.*

Not far from Arequipa, a man in one of the second class

carriages died very suddenly, they say, from consumption, poor man! & not a friend near him. It was a pitiful sight to see! At the next station officials put him in his poncho & lifted him up into a freight cart. We continued on our way up hills & round curves, until I, for one, was happy to alight at Arequipa, after a 172 miles journey, which took us 9 hours.

As usual it is feast day; anniversary of the independence, just like my luck, always a feast wherever I go. The town is a deserted comfortless looking place owing to the number of recent earthquakes. A nice Cathedral, all lighted by parafin "lamps", but the theatre all falling with no beauty about, the roof is of canvas all torn. The shops are poor but the English bazzar is good – acquaintances very limited but Doña Belisarda visited us & sent me cakes.

Next morning we rose by five o'clock to take the tram to the station for Puno. There are no cabs so Indians took the hand baggage.

No sooner had we started on our 13 hours ride when we went straight up to a height of 14,666 feet. We found the air very trying. Percy & I both ill with severe headache & difficulty in breathing. One poor man was so near eternity that he gasped for breath, & by dint of pills & strong smelling fluid, he was brought to his former state of health.

After a most tedious journey we arrived at Puno in the dark and grappled our way to the steamer. But oh! what a miserable prospect! For so many passengers only four cabins! And the two best were already engaged by four Engineers who are going out to Bolivia. Luckily the other two wretched cabins fell to our lot. Picture me, on the port side of the saloon about half a foot off the dining table in a cabin about half a yard in width from bed to wall, with four berths in it – each about 20 inches across, one above the other. Not room to dress, and to make one's toilet one has to go to the dining room and lift up the top of one of the tables with a cover over it in which a hole has been cut to reveal a hand basin (tin) saucer with soap & a nasty comb everybody uses; (during the day you are not allowed to wash). The cabin is so dark a candle is necessary even at midday, & as to cleanliness, that cannot be spoken of.

The cabin floor, I should say, has never been touched with water since new, & the paint, once white, is brown & black. The bed clothes have a strong odour.

After the passengers have dined, the room is turned into a bed room for men. Everything one touches is filthy, & most vulgar dishes. Lunch consisted of old, strong, *tinned salmon & meats, with strong raw onions on the top. The moment one descended to the dining saloon, the odour already disgusted one so much that immediately one got a glimpse of the table, it was "right about turn", to the deck again, with an empty stomach. Then to get to the deck one had to climb through a hole in the floor, about a yard sqr., with steep stairs & iron handrail black with dirt; the deck is filthy & no accommodation, not a seat nailed up. On the whole what with servants inattention etc. the steamer is disgusting.*

But the lake Titicaca itself is lovely: the water deep blue with lots of canoes made of straw, or long grass, dried and tied together; thick at one end and pointed at the other, exactly in the shape of a Turkish slipper turned up at the toes. In the distance are hills belonging to history where the Chilians exiled all the old Indians years ago. There are ruins of some old Inca buildings & tracks leading to cultivated terraces which keep the sand hills from falling as it is all very loose.

Although we arrived at Chililia at night, we were not permitted to disembark until six o'clock next morning. After another comfortless night we were all astir early & watching our luggage being hoisted on the small pier which runs out into the lake. It was a cold frosty morning, all white hoar & ice. Arriving at the custom house, the manager made himself disagreeable & started rummaging through all my boxes until the Prefect sent word to allow the Suarez's luggage to pass without examination.

Now ended the "water journey" & we began the old fashioned stage-coach travelling, drawn by eight mules, seats outside & in of the coach, no glass to the "would be windows" but india rubber curtains, & for back rest there were straps of leather.

We began at full speed with the mules & oh! the dust!

It came in the coach in clouds. We stopped for breakfast & to change mules. Then we trotted on & on again until quite unexpectedly we were met by Don Rodolfo & Don Belisario Barberi with a lovely "brake" & a pair of fine horses which we were glad to change into. We drove on in comfort until suddenly, to my surprize, we saw La Paz in the distance. It was down at the bottom of the mountains. What a hole to build a town in! & completely surrounded by mountains, the highest being "Illimani" which was covered with snow, and its shape & beauty stood out so clearly against the blue sky that one felt rooted to the spot in admiration. We began the descent to La Paz, but not without great fear & timidity on my part. Since we are up such a height, & the path is so narrow one thinks more about one's last day than about frivolity. Although the horses were prancing & appeared none too steady for such roads, thanks to a good N. American coachman, we wound down the mountain side – a distance of six miles – without injury. We were then driven through the streets to our rooms, already taken by the two said Gentlemen D. Rodolfo & D. Belisario, where we were left to rest & get over our excitement. Later the two gentlemen returned to take us out to dine.

Thus day by day passes: visitors, including the President's family, come dropping in twos by twos, until I have quite a large circul of acquaintance. Three months pass in La Paz: very pleasantly too, from the point of view of the outside world, but inside, one great disgust I have, which will be best left out.*

On the morning of the 26th November in a "Victoria" Pedro & I walked up to the coach-house for our departure from La Paz. It was more like a funeral than anything else. Our great friends the Velascos wept bitterly. Each put me on a escapulario so that my journey should be happy & prosperous. So we said "Good byes" & left the great town of Bolivia for smaller ones.

We drove up the mountain side "el alto" until, at the top, it seemed we were on one great plain like a great field without

---

* No doubt the discovery of another infidelity on the part of Don Pedro end. Then after two days & a half (doing 50 & 60 miles a day) we arrived in the "great Oruro" which we heard so much of, & found the most insignificant village: only one decent house in it, & that is Penny's* house. The only thing that makes the little place important are the mines of silver. One of these – belonging to Penny – we entered. Six of us each with our torch light. We walked as far as the machinery, almost three miles away; in some places the path was very narrow & low, & the air oppressive. Outside in the big yard, there were dozens of women breaking stones to seperate the good from the bad, that is to say, the most precious from the ordinary. We were all given pieces of ore.

The next part of our journey was very dangerous: the heights at which we travelled were terrific & we were completely at the mercy of the coachman. My greatest fear came when halfway down a mountain-side with an awful precipice & a river at the bottom, the mules began to rush full speed down the narrow rough stony path which one would scarcely call a road. Had a wheel come off or our Coachman been careless, we should have gone to the bottom. Fortunately having been scared at every turn, after going up then coming down some more enormous hills, we arrived in Cochabamba.

The ten days spent here were pleasant enough. We drove to Cala Cala, Quero-Quero, Muyurina, etc. etc. & enjoyed the sights; the countryside is very fertile & the fruit splendid, especially strawberries.

From Cochabambra we went by coach to Arani, this being our last ride on the way to Santa Cruz and our journey on mule back.

We started badly for the day was wet and we did only five leagues (15 miles). Most days we did as much as 45 to 50 miles a day. Sometimes the sun was so hot that we had to take refuge. When the rain came down heavily we covered ourselves with india rubber cloaks, but the mules would soon start slipping in the mud. My mule fell twice & threw me. I got a severe knock on the knee and tried to raise myself, but the

* Probably a gentleman named Peneranda.

My Bolivian Aunt

mud was so slippery that it was almost impossible. Fortunately my animal was very tame. Then Pedro came to my assistance (not with G.*) pulled my mule up the hill, while I tried to scramble up on foot & hands: even then I went one step forward & two behind. When I had time to look at my bruises I found I had a very swollen & black knee. However we journeyed on & that night a good old fatherly man sheltered us.

Next morning we rose at three o'clock & climbed a high mountain. When at day-break we had to start descending to Chilon I had to dismount three times, as the belly-band of my mule slackened & my saddle slipped into its neck.

Three days later at "Agua Blanca" I was taken frightfully ill with a terrible pain in the stomach: it began at 12 o'clock at night & lasted until 4 o'clock next day. Pedro was awfully scared. Two doctors attended me. I myself thought I should not live. When I felt a little better we mounted, & began the journey again. After about two leagues we went in search of medicines.

We journeyed on without more trouble & enjoyed the immense scenery and those woods & paths lined with white flowers; some maidenhair fern plants were like a gooseberry bush so high & bushy.

From Pampa Grande we journey to Samaipata where fresh mules & servants awaited us to take us on to Santa Cruz. From hereon the roads were so bad that it was impossible to climb & descend mounted. I did most of the journey on foot. Notwithstanding I fell twice. There were jumps of 2 yds. high Some mules put their four feet together & slid down. Others danced about without the courage to leap. With the help of a strong stick I was able to make my mule jump to safety.

One night the darkness came suddenly, & we had a very nasty rocky mountain to descend. My mule became so afraid of the darkness that it started to dance, & refused to jump over the stones, yet I had to give all my trust in my mule as I could not see my finger before me. Finally I dismounted, buckled the reins to my saddle, & drove the mule before me, & groped my

---

* Perhaps some lady in the party favoured by Pedro.

My aunt photographed in 1925, in her flat in Maida Vale.

No. 36 Rue Nicolas Ortiz.
Exterior of my aunt's house in Sucre.

(Above) The dining room of
my aunt's former house in Sucre.
(Right) A corner
of the drawing room.

way forward feeling with my feet & hands. Somehow or other we eventually arrived at the bottom.

Within 2 leagues from Santa X we were met by several men, relations & friends of Pedro's. There I changed my mule for a horse, & came on at full speed, up to the house of Manuel Suarez.

Here we lived till January 1892, then I moved to my Uncle Tomas Antonio S. Saucedo while Pedro was directing the building of a new road at Guitarras & suffered great hardship. I was cared for more than any daughter could be.

Well, I received visitors, dozens of them, for several weeks. Then we repaid the visits: people were very innocent & kind hearted. At three swell dances given at the Sorruco's, Serrates, & the Rinconada, I sang & was very much praised. After those nights it was always the same old tale "Will Mrs Suarez sing?" The favourite songs were "Juanita" & "La Golondrina".

But I forgot to mention from Jan. to April several things occurred. The first & most important was the revolution in Santa Cruz. This began Jan. 2nd. The revolutionists were Toledo, Ardaya, Otazo. We suffered their threats & insolence for one month, & then we "flew". Pedro, with several other foreigners were ready, & had all arranged to make the reaction when, unfortunately, the previous night one of the foreigners got drunk & shot one of the guards: with that accident, all was discovered. So we hurried Pedro away as quietly as we could. He had not gone more than a few hours when soldiers were sent to take him prisoner.

The day following, a proclamation was published that all young men above the age of 15 must present themselves to go & fight since regiments of the Collas were approaching. In order not to get mixed up in all this, we (Tio Tomas etc.) set out for the country at 2 o'clock in the morning Feb. 2.

How well I remember that scene! In dead silence we saddled our horses & mounted, the moon shining brightly before leaving the village. Any moment we quite expected to hear "Halt". But we got away without being interrupted altho many sleepless nights were passed as troops were sent out in search of us. Then we heard of the "Colla" troops, & how they had conquered & entered Santa X triumphantly. Gradually things calmed down, and eventually we returned to Santa X. We had been absent exactly speaking 22 days, from Feb. 2nd to 24th.

Then in April Constanza, the second daughter of Tio Tomas Suarez, was married to Don Jose Prada. Pedro & I were Padrinos. On the whole our time spent in Santa Cruz has been very pleasant.

When Pedro announced his intention to go to his home in the Beni, a dance was given as a "goodbye" gesture to him and as a birthday for me. I was very much celebrated with presents & bouquets of flowers from all parts (18 in all).

Three days later Pedro departed, but en route he met a friend who told him a boat was coming specially for him from his home. He returned, & resolved to take me with him.

On other occasions, the family had begged so fervently for him to leave me behind that he consented. But this time, he would not hear it. From the moment they all saw that Pedro was adamant they wept continually until we left. Poor things they are such good hearted people!

On the eve of my departure I was surrounded by all my friends – or rather a few of them – all wanting to touch me: some sat at my back, others in front & heaps at my side – all taking hold of my arms, hands, shoulders, etc. etc. I consoled them by saying I would be back in 3 months.

Well we set out, accompanied by men & women in all (mounted) about 40. It was a pretty sight to see. Our friends rode with us for about a league but a nasty small rain was falling & I told them to return before they were wet throughout. At last they left us to go on our journey.

While crossing a very strong & sandy river my horse overturned, & was almost drowned. It was saddled with my sleeping rugs on the seat, also a small bag with my keys. Well in all the scuffle my little bag was lost, & now all my boxes have had to be broken open! Just fancy! & on a journey where we cannot get keys or have them made!

Eventually I crossed that river in a hide, tied at the

corners, while two Indians pulled me. After that I had to mount
again & all my caronas & saddle was wet.

We arrived at Portachuelo in an awful state to find our
cargo had not arrived on account of the torrential rains. I was
without even a skirt to put on. But we soon made one & I
bought underlinen. We waited in that small village about 10
days before leaving for Cuatro Ojos. The next 27 miles were
awful! We went through mud & water that came up to the
horses belly. Where other horses fell my horse – a very tall one
– had its own step that was slow but it was sure. Were it not
that I am accustomed to the saddle I would have rolled off
several times. Once the horses fell, it was difficult to get their
legs free from the stickiness of the mud.

Before we came to the river journey, we had to take a
path where not only did the water come up to the horse's
saddle, but we had to stoop to avoid the spiky trees & thorns,
one of which, called the Holy tree, was full of ants that sting for
hours after they bite. To try to describe this part of the journey
is waste of time & paper so I shall leave it. I will only say that
eventually we arrived at the port of the River Piray where
we found our servants waiting with a boat ready to be loaded.
For seven days we travelled without many novelties. We left
Rio Grande on 1st of April & entered the Mamore.

The river in width & depth is enormous; the current is
at a rate of 4 miles an hour so that big trees are uprooted &
thrown down by the middle of the river like a big steamer.
There are many whirlpools, some are half a mile in length.
Every now & again we went aground on a sand-bank in the
middle of the river. All the men had to jump into the water
immediately or we should have had a good wetting ourselves.

(Note) I forgot to mention about the New Year's Carnival
in Santa Cruz being one of the most enjoyable feasts of all
the year round. For several weeks beforehand the women sewed
at their costumes. As there are no professional dressmakers
necessity makes one "set to". We (Eliza, Zoraida Suarez & I)
made 12 more dresses of not great value, but prettily trimmed
& adorned with laces, while the men, taking as much trouble

as the ladies, were busy buying up all the pretty materials (chiefly velvet) for fancy costumes.

At last the carousal started. There were "societies" in different colours – such as the "Curate Society" in pure white with tall pointed hats, then the "Evening drilldress society" in pure white drill, with opera hats, with old Grand Father (I might call him Grand Father Christmas as he certainly represented him & no other) heading the society who all walked in troops of about 12 to 16 men.

From the far end of the village arrived two brass bands, followed by many carriages. There were dozens, nay! I may say hundreds – on horseback with one leading the whole regiment. It was of course no other than Pedro! I was on a balcony which gave us a splendid view.

Later I had to dress the hair of nearly all the Cousins for the dance to be given the same evening. As the usual fashion is to wear the hair in one or two plaits, & only on very rare occasions is it coiffed, it fell to my lot being the most expert to comb 13 that evening. Up till the last moment I was busy. However, I managed, & was ready by nine o'clock, donned a spring green silk covered with fine white lace caught up with pale pink ribbons & bunches of pale pink rose buds, which was said to be the most effective, & I really thought so myself.

The dance was crowded since there were at least three hundred present. With the masked or disguised men one had to be very careful. I, as a rule, treated all with reserve.

The wines, ices, chicken & "Ambigu" were excellent, & there were two very good brass bands (no piano). The ball finished about five o'clock.

Next day being Carnival Sunday we were dressed in our "Sunday best" to await the "comparsas". Several "Societies" engage bands, then make their rounds to all the favourite houses. Here they dance, & play the fool with tubes of perfume & confetti (by the way! it is most difficult to get out of the hair), and after about an hour there is a general "clear out" & then another "comparsas" arrives, & so on from the Sunday until the Wednesday.

Of course every night there was a big ball, so one may

imagine how tiring it was to dance all day, then to prepare, & dance enthusiastically all night for three & four days. And the new dresses one required was no small trifle! Yet, from the beginning to the end it was one of the most jolly times I ever spent, & shall never forget.

(End of note)

Since we arrived in Santa X up till today (April 3rd), I have not taken down any notes of what has passed. This I attribute to the merry time I have passed.

In August we had the merry festivities for the anniversary of the independence of Bolivia.

The "Filarmonica" society celebrated with a full dress Ball held at the Tia Narica. The Patio was arranged in a very pretty & uncommon style, with its six pillars on each side of the corredo *hung with the Bolivian flag while lace curtains and lamps hung between each pillar. One idea, which I gave them, looked even nicer than I expected: at the foot of each pillar we placed a small table with vases full of exquisite & fragrant flowers: two on each table & a lamp between. There were 20 tables & 40 flower vases, so imagine the scent! The young ladies had used exquisite taste in their dresses, altho it was publicly said I was the best dressed. I wore salmon coloured pongee covered with black chenile spotted net.*

They were jolly days that passed, (with the exception of a great disgust that was passed between Pedro & another married woman). But they ended with the preparations for our journey to Mojos. Before leaving Pedro suggested we should give a concert to benefit the hospital. So all hands to work. We got up a "Lirico-Dramática Funcion" the following Sunday. Two peti-piesa, music, & singing. I sung three times, first song "Diamates de la Corona", "Loves golden dream", "El Quillo de Hierro". It was so very much liked that the village asked us to repeat it. So for three nights it was repeated & that was the last "fuss" we made before leaving Santa Cruz.

After nearly two & a half years of travel Pedro and I were at last about to enter the capital of the Beni. The prefect of the Beni, Samuel Portales, in an attempt to reorganize the country, has decided to make the "fat fry the lean". He has

E*

stolen men & women servants from all the "better-off", imposed taxes on travellers, and created great difficulties for those who have been clever enough to make a go of the natural resources of the rich countryside. As we approached Trinidad we wondered what treatment was in store for us.

During our four days visit, we lodged in the late Tio Antonio rooms. Many people came to see us, but some of Pedro's relations appeared very cool on account of his mixing in political affairs. We were quite glad to leave for Santa Ana. Well Santa Ana was rather a "damper" to me. It was pouring with tropical rain & I found everybody so cool & reserved, the village was awfully ruined, & all was abominable. Another reason for my dislike was that we were staying only one block from Pedro's mother, where we had to go for our meals daily. Another objection: in the evening the sun was very hot. Santa Ana never was a favourite place of mine.

As luck would have it, after six weeks residence, we left the place. Pedro resolved to go on urgent business back to Santa Cruz. Arrangements were soon made, we said goodbye to all & left in a small boat: Pedro and I with six oarsmen.

We rowed down the river Yapacani until we arrived at the mouth of the Mamore at which point we now had to row up river. At San Pedro we slept on the playa, or river bank while a tiger* growled round us all night: I felt rather afraid.

At Tambuen a Sr Chavez was stationed with his steamer at-the-ready to sail. All he needed were engineers & good practical men who could navigate the rivers. We took on board a "run away" from a supposed revolution in Trinidad, & a friend of Pedro's, Dr Cubertino.

At this point of the journey there were many sandbanks – good for sleeping on. One night a strong south wind rose & blew our mosquito nets up in the air. At daybreak we found ourselves covered from head to toe with sand about an inch thick. Our bed-clothes were the colour of the sand. We were in

* There are, in fact, no tigers in Bolivia. The cougar (also known as puma) is to be seen in the Beni area, though the jaguar is the largest feline in the Americas, and is found in many habitats, but prefers river banks where it sleeps by day and hunts at dusk. It shows no fear of man and may become a 'man-eater'. Most South Americans refer to it as *tigre*.

a filthy state. I was glad to dress quickly and get out of the mess. The wind was piercing. The flood of the last two days has somehow affected the water we drink & cook with. It has become simply mud. It is impossible to wash a rag.

Last night we slept very restlessly on a playa for as soon as we alighted from our boats we heard a drum beaten, quite near. We imagined it was the savages calling their relations to begin to fight with us. So I arranged a bed on board while the men slept on shore. We fired several shots, & to our surprise we were answered by others higher up the river: we knew travellers were near & early next morning two boats arrived at our sand-bank, bringing a poor little dead child with them. The girl had died through the night from hooping cough, & the poor Mother was in a sad state.

The next evening we came to the mouth of the Yapacani river, slept there & next morning at dawn entered the Mio Para. Here we saw, close to the river on the sand-bank, a lovely tiger, the first I have seen so near. We arrived at Paila & arranged small canoa *to go on before us to explore. We gave the men their food for six days only so that they must return quickly.*

One evening we heard the sound of pigs teeth gnawing. The two men (Pedro & D. Cubertino) jumped on land, gun in hand, & saw a troop of about 400. They chased them some distance. After an absence of three hours & a long run they were lost in a wood. The two men went so far that the shots of their guns could not be heard by us on the river. I was becoming worried when they returned with five pigs – exhausted, tired, hungry, flesh torn, by the thorns, but grand sport they had had. As the sun was fast sinking we rowed to the opposite side of the river & there skinned the pigs & cut them in pieces; then put on chapapas *for the roast. We had a splendid meal. After a nightcap cup of chocolate, we retired to our sand-bank beds & slept until about 4 o'clock when we were awoken by our companion D.C. quietly informing us savages were near. He had heard their footsteps in the wood. I dressed quickly & made for the boat while Pedro & D.C. stood their ground. I sent them bullets from the boat & then they fired shots towards the noises they heard. As it was still dark & Pedro & D.C. could not see anything, they listened to the footsteps & discovered that the savages were divided into two troops, one above & the other below us. They obviously intended to take us & surround us on all parts.*

We were on very dangerous ground, & near to our last moments. Had our companion not heard them in time, the savages would have torn us into pieces. But as luck would have it, our time had not arrived to quit this world.

The servants bundled up our beds & belongings, & we all sat in our boat awaiting day-break. Had we moved, we should have been in greater danger, as the "Sirionos" (these troops of savages are so called) would have attacked us in an even more advantageous place. When at daybreak we left, we expected the savages would follow us all day since the journeying up river is very slow & difficult, (& we realised we could not escape down river), but mercifully we were not molested – even when we stopped for a meal.

The following night we chose – not without great care – a position on the opposite side of the river. We preferred pigs to savages. As to myself, I never closed my eyes – nor for several nights afterwards.

At daybreak we rowed on until eventually we arrived at "La Cruz del Obispo", but dared not stay the night for it is considered the most dangerous place from the point of view of savages. So we rowed on until it was too dark to run the risk of continuing since the flooded river was full of tree trunks.

Since all these recent excitements I have become so nervous that I decided to sleep alone in the tiny cabin while the rest were on shore. In the middle of the night I was awoken by a peculiar cry & this cry was answered from far. I went to awake Pedro. Soon afterwards we heard from the wood close by footsteps crushing the dead leaves & sticks, so once more P. & Don C. listened with gun in hand. It turned out that either we, or they were not in a very advantageous position, so the savages decided not to shoot their arrows, neither did the men fire their guns.

I sat on deck, wrapped up in rugs, until day-break. Only those who have experienced such feelings & passed such nights as these can imagine our thoughts!

A cold chilly night it was with dew falling fast. Our nerves were strung up to listen to every sound. We did not know from where or at what moment the savages might advance upon us Oh! such sleepless nights those were! Fearing anything would happen to Pedro or his companion – for without them the women would be lost; the Indians are a very cowardly set: as soon as danger is near they jump into the water & leave the Patron *or Master to defend himself: so it is "everybody for himself".*

Before leaving at daylight we saw on the sand-bank the quite fresh foot-prints of the savages. Evidently they had been awaiting us.

The Piray river, especially in the wet season, is one of the most dangerous in all Bolivia: it has swallowed many lives & fortunes in its strong current; big trees have been swept down it, or buried by the whirlpools. It varies in depths so much that in some parts one cannot fathom it, but we now found the river so shallow that we had to take out about 51 arrobas (about 95 stone) & leave them hidden in a wood at Ecquichoma. Thinking that with so much less cargo we could manage to continue, we found our mistake. We had to empty the boat completely, & put everything in the "pelota" (the hides tied at the corners & made into a sort of square oven tin-shape,) & then drag them with the men walking in the water. Our boat was now empty except for a few eatables. The three men servants & two women servants with P. & D.C. with the aid of long sticks then managed the boat with just one in it.

It was only when we reached "El Asunta" that we felt that the savages had decided to leave us to go our own way, not by boat for the river is so low, but by pelotas. With our arrival in "Cuatro Ojos" we are at the end of our river journey. Here I remained in the port several days while the servants returned with Pedro to bring back the cargo we had left behind.

My Bolivian Aunt

On the second day I had a dreadful attack, stomach ache & pains in the bowels, that made me take to my bed. However I got from bed to horse-back, & mounted for a three days' trek. Each day we trotted 40 miles for 9 hours until we arrived back here in Santa at midnight. There was hearty greeting & a regular big circul of people to welcome me.

13 Assessment

This one surviving diary indicates that my aunt would never have been a rival to Rosita Forbes or, through her literary efforts, have made a fortune. But it does show that it is more than likely that her 'tall stories' were, in fact, based on the truth. In all probability she had made the acquaintance of Colonel Fawcett, had jumped for her life up a tree when chased by a bull, and felt the breath of a jaguar on her face. During the twenty-two years that she spent in South America, she was no doubt involved in many interesting events and faced quite a number of dangers. Again I wondered how on earth I could have been so lax, and lacking in human interest, as not to beg her to give me her first-hand reports on all her adventures. Why did I never ask her how it came about that she realized Don Pedro was the man who could give her the life she wanted?

By now few people remained to re-tell her travellers' tales. My mother seemed more reticent, difficult of approach, and vague than ever. My Aunt Cada explained that Jessie, being fifteen years older than herself, had only been known well to her after her final return from Sucre. Yet, as the years passed, the memory of Aunt Jessie did not fade, and not only would she reappear in nostalgic family reminiscences, but her surprising reactions would be applied to all sorts of current situations. Many of her catch-phrases continued to be used: 'It's just so much nothing,' 'It is and it isn't,' still had their uses. But perhaps it was watching others who had once been admired and pampered, and had later discovered their inability to adjust themselves to old age and misfortune, that made me realize that my aunt was, in this particular way, quite remarkable. Rather than dispersing with the passage of time, the awareness of her exceptional qualities became ever stronger.

For some while, following the death of my aunt, my work as a designer in the theatre took precedence over other activities; whenever a production of some Victorian or Edwardian film or play was planned, it would seem that I was called upon. At Cambridge I had come under the influence of the Victorians and, without being too immodest, I consider that I was one of the first to do pastiches of their styles which, by degrees, caught the popular taste. Then my inspiration came from the Edwardians, and over-upholstered furniture, palms in pots, and women with up-do hair and hourglass waists came back on to the scene. In the early 'sixties it was almost inevitable that all musical comedies, and indeed most play-revivals, no matter when they were written, were mounted, particularly in New York, in a vaguely Edwardian style.

With *My Fair Lady* came the chance to do something in the 1912 period. Perhaps we always like best the fashions just before our own time – those that we first saw with the rose-coloured vision of childhood, so it is not surprising that I loved the pre-World War One taste for Louis XVI trellis-work rooms, cane-backed chairs with grey-painted, carved swags on which sat Canova-like goddesses in the latest versions of Empire-waisted dresses. This period fitted perfectly the date of Shaw's *Pygmalion* on which our musical was based, so when the management wanted me to do the production in Edwardian costume I made a strong plea for the later date. But the management was worried: 'Will these clothes have any sex appeal?' Promises were made that they would.

I started on the job with a passionate relish, knowing that I had such a rich fount of knowledge to work on. From Act One, with the ladies from the opera in their high-collared, tasselled opera-cloaks with 'art-deco' trimmings, to Ascot and the Ball, the costumes were dividends from my study of life at No. 74 Compayne Gardens. It was Madame Triana in the marquee at one of my aunt's garden parties, in pearl-grey satin with a gigantic grey hat of ostrich feathers, who gave me the clue as to how Mrs Higgins should be dressed at the races. Many of the hats were copies of Madame Jandrot's creations and came straight out of Aunt Jessie's huge, shining black trunks. Certainly I had in mind the baskets of artificial flowers from the Mesdames Lespiaut when ordering the cart-wheels of Parma violets, the full-blown roses, and the lilies-of-the-valley to be tucked into the ladies' waistbands. Perhaps a little of the star-dust fell on to my designs from the sequined concoctions that the private dressmaker ran up in my aunt's converted spare-bedroom-workshop.

In creative work of almost every kind, one of the most important prerequisites is that the artist should have enjoyed himself. This is particularly the case with a theatre designer: the public can always sense it if he has relied upon technique only. It pleases me to think that my enjoyment at re-creating my adolescent enthusiasms was sensed by the *Fair Lady* audiences. Certainly my family recognized the origins of many of my effects, and when, during the first night in London, various characters appeared in hobble-skirts, over-size aigretted hats and chinchilla muffs, they laughed: 'Why, it's just Aunt Jessie all over again!'

My Fair Lady led to my doing several other productions in the fashions of the pre-World War I period. Each time I started off on my designs I knew that Aunt Jessie was at my elbow to help me. Time passed, and I found myself in many varied parts of the world, yet the presence of my aunt remained strong. Perhaps she was still at the back of my mind when, one September evening, I was motoring through a small mountain village in the Dordogne and stopped to ask the way of three women sitting by a well-head, doing their needlework and gossiping before dusk fell. Two of these women were particularly ugly and quite sullen; but the third, who gave me the necessary instructions with an obvious enjoyment and unusual verve, was a reincarnation of Aunt Jessie. Her eyes were adorned with the same puffs of amusement that are shown in a portrait of Diane de Poitiers or Nell Gwynn, and her sable-brown hair was pulled up in a shapelessness that is seldom seen today. She appeared exactly like the young Jessie Sisson when photographed in Cumberland with the arm of her fiancé protectively placed on her shoulder. It was only when I had driven on, and the light had failed, that I wondered why I had not taken a snapshot. During the remainder of my time in the Dordogne I tried to find this same young woman, but even the village eluded me.

Back in London some while later, I decided I would take another look at 'Santa Cruz'. One morning, walking along West End Lane, I recognized the high, red brick walls of Compayne Gardens topped with bushes of dark, greasy euonymous, and turned down towards No. 74. There appeared the Alberdi mansion of grey stone, but it seemed to be half its size. I discovered that it had been turned into apartments, with a row of buttons, and cards stating the present occupiers' names at the front door; a geyser was seen at the window of Madame Alberdi's former Louis XIV drawing room. But where was No. 74? I was trying to find some relic of its former existenec when two foreigners stopped in their car and asked if they could help me. I explained that where now there was a hideous block of modern flats, there used to be a house . . .

'Oh, that's gone long ago!'

They both laughed ghoulishly; the progress of life was of great amusement to them. They drove off.

The new, impersonal honeycomb of cement, with its life-less windows, completely obliterated the past. But a narrow passage led to the rear of the building: I walked down it. The back quarters were where the modern architect had placed the lavatories and kitchens. The cramped, low windows displayed tins and packets of Omo, Persil, Parozone, Tide and Harpic. On a shelf by a sink a sunflower, made of felt in a twee pot, purported to augur the changes of the weather outside.

Sadly shrunk and small, but still in fair repair, was Aunt Jessie's erstwhile garden. The rockery – which had been made of stones that looked like petrified spittle – had been flattened; gone was the glass-house where she had nurtured the orchids that reminded her of the Bolivian jungle. There was nothing recognizable left now but the may trees and the lawn; everything else had changed.

14 Peru

Having been prevented from having a summer holiday by a protracted theatrical ordeal on Broadway, I decided to celebrate the year 1970 by taking a winter vacation and visiting some country for the first time – like Peru, for instance, or Bolivia. Sam Green, a modern art curator from Philadelphia, without a Philadelphian trait but with enormous enthusiasm, had recently visited these countries and suggested that, if I decided to make the journey, he would like to return. It would be an opportunity to discover for myself the continent on which my Aunt Jessie had developed her highly rouged personality and rugged strength of character. Thus, with Sam as my travelling companion, I embarked upon my '*à la recherche de la tante perdue*'.

From the moment of landing from the air on Latin American tarmac, I found myself looking around, perhaps unconsciously, for traces of Aunt Jessie. Even at Lima airport, as they welcomed their long-lost friends or relations, I recognized a black-dressed group of just the same blueish-skinned men and magnolia-complexioned women who had amazed me at my aunt's house as a child. Quite of a sudden I remembered that some of them, too, had had yellow whites to the mahogany irises of their eyes. That gentleman nodding mechanically with the 'one way' smile was surely a member of the Suarez family; those ladies with their flamboyant greetings, the leaning forwards, or tilting backwards or sideways of the head, and so profusely kissing one another on both cheeks, might well have been from some branch of the Alberdi tree; the same good-natured family laughter had surrounded my aunt half a century ago. I was pleased that, even in an ultra-modern and extremely elegant airport, nothing so basic as human characteristics and manners was any different.

Certainly nothing had changed in the arid, mountainous desert – apart from the *autostrada* on which we drove towards the city. This was a dour world where it never rains and nothing grows: a scene of alarming barrenness. Everything was dust-coloured and dry. A few solitary figures could be seen, hunched close to the parched landscape in an attempt to escape from the scorching wind or sun.

Nearing the city, the biscuit desolation gave signs of industrial life with derricks, mine shafts, and pylons all coated with the uniform drabness of dust. It was as if the spectrum had been broken and only a colourless world presented itself.

Then we came to the terrible slum dwellings, the *Barrieras*. The roofless mud shacks, where three hundred thousand human beings are crowded together, spread like leprosy over a large hilly area with almost no sewage or water supply; all varieties of disease are rampant and police are impotent to combat violence and crime. It is inconceivable that the inhabitants, having originally migrated from the clean air of fertile plains or from the luxuriant forests, should prefer to remain in this tuberculosis-ridden squalor in danger of earthquakes; yet, in spite of every inducement, they do not wish to move.

As one motored towards Lima it became apparent that even here nature persisted, and that by irrigation, amid this utter desolation, vegatables could be made to grow. In fact, as one neared the outskirts of the city it was surprising to find that the grass was as vivid, and the trees just as feathery and lush, as in a French Impressionist landscape. In this formerly parched wasteland, by artificial means the earth had been forced to yield the best of food. In many parts of Peru, man's mastery over his habitation is impressive.

The flowering suburb of Miraflores is well-named, for beds of calla lilies, cannas and geraniums are planted down the centre of the thoroughfares. This was the grand residential section where the houses were kept hidden behind hibiscus and frangipani trees, and where, at the turn of the century, my uncle and aunt joined the cavalcade of fashion as the carriages circumnavigated the *avenidas* lined with palm and poinsettia. Lima was the seat of the Viceroy, and the Limaens in their carriages were conscious of their self-importance. Rich beyond belief, they considered themselves the cream of society, speaking the purest Spanish in the whole of South America. Many of the houses, reminiscent of New Orleans, had verandahs of elaborate wrought-iron work on tall, decorative struts running around their four sides. Here, to avoid the heat, the luxurious women spent most of the day in fluffy negligées sitting on their wicker-work chairs, preserving their magnolia complexions and buffing their nails with a pink powder, while the four of five dependant aunts, in black sat telling their beads. A parrot on a stand would join in the monotony of the prayers; then occasionally, out of appalling boredom, it would let out an ear-splitting squawk and a series of burps, followed by a succession of swear words. At five o'clock in the evening the menfolk returned, and the formal salon would be used, the chairs placed in rows around the walls, and in the centre of the room a table, on which stood a cut-glass vase contained a peacock's tail display of flowers.

Other large villas in Miraflores were built in stone in an amorphous *opéra bouffe* style, and it was fitting that in one of these Hispanic-Franco mansions, 'La Perichole' had doubtless entertained at supper the sexy sexagenarian Viceroy after she had received a standing ovation for her acting in the latest play of Lope da Vaga.

But it was sad to notice that, today, most of these houses were empty or had seen better days. Even here everything was coated with layers of dust, and no one was to be seen on verandah or at unwashed window. Only the modern streets of Miraflores seemed inhabited, but these one-storey buildings are of a labour-saving design and bereft of all character.

The general effect of shabbiness increased as we neared the capital city, where the great octagons and squares had been laid out with a pride that had now taken a fall, and the former architectural hauteur of imposing club buildings, with their colonnaded porticos and sweeping staircases, had been jarred by the encroaching ubiquity of advertising. Posters were stuck on to noble walls, neon lights flashed over grandiose porticos, and above the general din of traffic, roving loud-speakers made their deafening demands for participation in the national sweepstake. Across the square by the cathedral came the spearhead of the latest demonstration by Peruvian youth with banners proclaiming against the censorship of the Press.

In the days when my aunt went shopping, the vast general stores were German-owned, the Italians had coined the grocers' market, and France sent her foremost fashion experts to run the millinery business. The best of its kind from all over the world could be found here. The Hotel Maury, where my aunt stayed, was filled with rich Americans and English who were running the railways, or with singers or dancers enticed by the vast salaries offered for one appearance at the Opera House.

It was here in 1917 that the ten-year-old Fredrick Ashton first saw Pavlova. He considered her the most beautiful creature he had ever seen, and for days afterwards waited at the stage door to catch another glimpse of the star. Freddie recently described the strict conventionality and absurdity of Limaen society. He told of an afternoon reception, given in honour of Pavlova, at which only the men materialized. When the *ballerina-assoluta* realized the absence of the ladies she threw teacup and saucer to the ground, stormed out of the room, and went off to create a sensation in the newspapers. None-theless, Peruvian society continued, throughout and long after the Great War, to remain completely self-contained, and un-affected by almost anything serious that happened in the rest of the world. It was the same little group of people who, to avoid the heat of the city, went to Ancon, the local Deauville. In the foggy months of winter they met again in the mountains of Chosica where, as the train arrived, they were greeted by flower sellers offering bunches of violets the size of a plate.

Today in Lima there are only a few traces of this lost world. The baroque banks, with their plate glass doors, are still in use, and the lobby of the Gran Hotel Simon Bolivar, with its liver-coloured marble columns and palm trees, is busy with frantic *concierges,* scurrying bell-boys, and arrivals and departures.

In the garish splendour of the Palace the recently appointed President, formerly a revolutionary general, rationalizes
his work, stressing that his rebellion had been necessary for
the economy of the country, and with histrionic gestures warning that his government would brook no interference from
outside; he is willing to be friendly with countries who agree
with his reforms to reduce private riches and ease public
poverty, and he welcomes tourist trade. He waves his arm as
he talks of 'the new Peru'. A note of dramatic reality is struck
when the English interpreter becomes faint and is taken, semi-
conscious, to the window for fresher air.

A few families still live in old colonial houses, built around
large courtyards (since it never rains, they are open to the sun
and the stars). They are still privileged enough to be served by
a handful of grinning family servants. But they live in anxiety
that, at any moment, their remaining interests are to be taken
from them. In secret they criticize the way the government,
inexperienced in such matters, interferes, 'with disastrous
results,' in the few remaining successful industries.

But how amusing it was to discover that in the decoration
and furnishings of these houses, restaurants, and antique
shops, the familiar was everywhere. The Indian rugs, woven
in stripes of orange and reds, the chests, the caskets, were the
contents of my aunt's rooms! Here were her ornate 'mara'
colonial-framed looking-glasses, incredibly ornate with their
gilded carvings in an infinite variety of designs: some with
lumps of mirror encased – like cherries in nougat – among the
diamond or honeycomb patterns. Here was her collection –
both authentic and in modern copies – of the powdery gold
wooden candlesticks, and the bowls, beakers and trays of
Potosi silver. Most familiar of all were the Cuzco School of
paintings, on copper, of crucifixion scenes, or portraits of
martyrs and saints, and the Madonna, with pear-shaped tears,
in stiff, triangular skirts standing on a naïf crescent of bulbous
roses.

At the 'Tombo di Oro', originally a sprawling dwelling

built (on one level, against earthquakes) for a family of thirteen brothers, a huge dinner party was given in honour of the President of Braniff Airlines which brings most of the tourists to Peru. It was enjoyable to watch the easy familiarity and the florid manners of the gentlemen and the flirtatious response of the ladies; this was just how the 'girls and boys' had behaved whenever my aunt invited a group of friends to her house. 'Here is one of the most beautiful women in all Peru,' our host was introducing a plump little pullet in a beaded pillow case and hennaed Marie Antoinette hair. The dimpled lady wagged her head coquettishly from side to side and displayed her huge brown eyes in an exaggerated *oeuillade*; but she was not as beautiful as the pigeony Beatrice Alberdi. 'Here is another very lovely lady.' Bigger eyes, more dimples. 'And here is the belle of Lima.' No – this time our host had gone too far!

It is known that well-favoured South American ladies take a considerable time to prepare themselves for public display (the finished product is always acclaimed with the admiration and respect it demands), so no one was surprised that it was almost two hours after they were bidden that many of the guests arrived. I now remembered that at Compayne Gardens nobody ever hurried, and punctuality was never considered a challenge.

For this gala, patio after patio was filled with tables set with fine silver and cut-glass goblets, and a hundred dozen flesh-pink roses, of the variety I had seldom seen since my aunt's day, were arranged at the tables in the formal style of the Victorian era. The 'Tombo di Oro' seemed to be an oasis in the centre of contemporary life. A descendant of one of the thirteen brothers, an attractive girl who had been born in one of these rooms, wore the 'farthest out' of gear, with a necklace of gold, crystal and turquoise that had been made two thousand years before Christ. Towards dawn this attractive girl took us to the latest discothèque, where the young Limaens groove away in a décor that is as 'cool' and snappy as anything of its sort in Paris or New York.

My aunt, with her unflagging curiosity, would have wandered through the palatial rooms of the Decorative Arts Museum, beguiled by the charm and fantasy of the most uncomfortable colonial furniture; but many of the exhibits are seen today under a layer of dust. The shabbiness creates a deadness, and if Aunt Jessie were alive it would be to the Herrera Museum that she would go. Here the pots and animals and effigies are piled in rows so high that many of the remarkable works of primitive art are impossible to see. Aunt Jessie would have been duly impressed by the grandeur of the royal robes made entirely of kingfisher feathers, the astonishing textures of textiles, the black pottery of the Chimu, the red of the Mochica, and the quantity and quality of relics of one culture after another. But the *Checcan* – the Quechan word for 'love', meaning pornographic – collection would have caused her to exclaim: 'Orch-ta-taie!' and sent her hurrying away in disgust. These little burial figures, illustrating scenes from everyday life, prove that every sexual perversity associated with a decadent society had been considered quite natural to a primitive people.

But if only my aunt, with her love for the Inca, could have seen the Gold Museum! This has only recently been donated to the country by the collector, Sr Miguel Mojica. It is a marvellously dramatic illustration of the ways in which gold can be used when it is admired for its beauty, its glitter, its glamour, more than for its monetary value. The presentation is superb, using jewel-coloured velvets as backgrounds for different-coloured golds in necklaces like wreaths of leaves, chandelier-earrings, goblets and beakers, sacrificial knives, sandals, ear-plugs, animal statues, and death masks. Here are the breastplates and coronation crowns of kings, flecked with a hundred lights from the dangling, paper-thin coins with which the crowns are decorated. The craftsmanship and bold simplicity of design give them a contemporary quality which adds to the aura of mystery.

It was in Cuzco that my aunt spent most of her time in Peru. That she loved the town with its Cyclopean stone-walled streets and temples was obvious from the way its name sounded on her lips like a kiss. Cuzco suited the ingenuous, childlike taste of my aunt, with her acceptance of all that glitters as real gold. Just like the wild-looking creatures down from the mountain to sell their wares, she was completely overwhelmed by the grandeur of the cathedral with its barley-sugar columns, silver altars, side chapels with guttering tallow candles, the realistic, enamel-painted carvings of figures in the throes of ecstasy or torture, and the sentimental, rosy-cheeked Madonnas in bridal white satin and lace veils.

Aunt Jessie delighted in the 'sugar and spice' baroque Spanish churches which were superimposed on the ruins of the bold and imposing Inca monuments. Pelion on Ossa, gilt on gingerbread: some people may be critical of this rollicking exuberance, emotional robustness, and unrestrained taste; but it is to the taste of the Cholos with their love of shrines, images and ceremonies, and my aunt loved it too. No doubt in her day these churches were kept up in a worthy state; but time and the decline of wealth has wrought great damage, the gilt and paintings are in a poor state of preservation, and the cheap, imitation-silk altar-cloths stained and in holes. Beneath the gold altar-piece a row of milk bottles is filled with half-dead gladioli; a long flex terminates in an open electric light bulb placed in the hand of a beckoning angel; strips of exposed neon lighting are used to illuminate a Madonna's shrine or the cadaver of a saint.

My aunt was doubtless wakened, just as we were, soon after dawn, by a burst of rockets and fire crackers. Still half-asleep, she would wonder if these explosions signalled the start of another revolution, then realize that some young Indian boys were playing the same old game of which they never tire. Wide awake, she could not waste the early morning in sleep and, with a veil over her dark red hair, would hurry off to pray – not in the great cathedral but, probably, in the intimate cosiness of the Church of San Domingo. This church has been built on the site of the ancient Temple of the Sun, made all of gold, even the thatch of gold spikes (the Temple of the Moon had been all in silver).

After saying her prayers, she would climb down the steep

flights of stone steps and, on her way past the shops which, by now were beginning to display their offerings, she could not resist buying another llama fur rug – red, black and white – for Welby's motor car, for covers on the brass beds, or for gifts to our family. The feel of these soft fronds of fur in the nostrils takes me back beyond the limit of memory. In Cuzco, too, she bought her vicuña scarves and handwoven rugs of brilliant stripes, and the embroidered Spanish shawls that no one admired in England.

It was during Doña Leticia's last years in Latin America that she heard of the American explorer, Hiram Bingham, and of how, leaving his companions to remain below collecting butterflies, he clambered through the clouds to the great bergs of black mountain, to make his marvellous discovery of Maccu Piccu which even the gold-ravenous Spanish had missed. Aunt Jessie was determined to see this great fortress, one of the wonders of the world; but for once Pedro was adamant in his refusal to allow her to leave Cuzco to face the ascent of fifteen thousand feet above the Urabamba River which, even today, is a feat of endurance. Aunt Jessie had to console herself with the reports of travellers who described to her the Sacred Palace, the temples built in worship of the Sun God and the Sun Maidens, the storehouses, private dwellings, and look-out forts against which no enemy would even attempt to advance. And like us, she marvelled that these giant stones could have been brought to this particular mountain summit when the Inca had no wheel. How could they have been placed with such incredible precision without the use of mortar? And who could have architected these flights of hanging-terraces or *andenes*? Maccu Piccu is a feat of unparalleled skill and a fitting memorial to the genius of the Inca.

15 *Bolivia III*

am Green, with his prior knowledge of Bolivia, was more equipped than I to make air and car arrangements for the continuation of our journey. But, in spite of telegrams sent confidently in all directions, we discovered that, once no longer under the hospitable wing of the reliable Braniff, plans would as often as not be baulked by some small airline cancelling the flight on the next leg of our trip. Quite a sheaf of unused air tickets, to places whose names were familiar since my childhood, filled our pockets; alternative plans and accommodation had to be devised. Sam's talent for ingenuity was put to severe tests, and sometimes even he became a little deflated by unforeseen difficulties. Another of his frustrations arose from the fact that Sam is an inveterate sightseer and a serious shopper: he could never discover the hours when the doors of churches and museums would be unlocked – nor why we always arrived in some remote mountain town on early closing day. By sometimes painful or frustrating, though often delightful, degrees we made our discovery of Bolivia.

I had come to this country in almost total ignorance of its long and violent history; since the Incas had no written language it is difficult to learn much about the Chavin, Chimu and earlier cultures whom they conquered, whose myths they proceeded to obliterate, and whose 'false' gods they deposed.

However, we do know that the Quechan-speaking Incas, who originally claimed to be 'The Sons of the Sun' were, in fact, simple llama-herders who came from the Cuzco uplands about the year 1100. They soon subordinated the few remaining Cholos living among the ruins of the gigantic, Stonehenge-like megaliths of Tiahuanaco which can be seen in and around La Paz today. During their brief history Bolivia became so

Aunt Jessie and her candidum lilies, at Broadchalke in Wiltshire, June, 1949.

Left to right: Madame Aramayo, Princess Glorietta and Jessie Suarez.
This was a photograph shown to me in Sucre in 1970.

rich that its fabled streets of gold and silver sheeting were the magnet for the greed of the barbarian.

The Inca rulers were ruthless – austere, humourless and proud – but their honesty and solid belief in the goodness of others was their undoing. When the soldier-peasant Pizarro presented himself to the King Atahulpa as a friend, in the name of Christ, the Inca trusted the Spaniard. With his gesture of flinging down his handkerchief as a sign for the slaughter to begin, the Spaniard became not so much a Conquistador as the despicable destroyer of a noble empire and the personification of evil in man. After his initial act of perfidy (almost to a man the Incas were massacred and, after a farcical trial, King Atahulpa was garrotted) the loathsome Pizarro continued a policy of wanton desecration, and proved himself incapable of any administrative skill. The Spanish atrocities in Peru, and Pizarro's massacre of the Incas, can only be compared to those of the Germans from the time of Attila to the horrors of the Nazi regime.

How could the Indians become assimilated into the colonial way of life when treated with nothing but senseless brutality? A quiet, but dogged resistance to two centuries of Spanish misrule culminated in the inevitable overthrow, and the Independence of Bolivia on 25 May 1809.

Bolivia has more than her share of natural resources, from sea level to a height of twenty thousand feet. In her fertile valleys, jungles, rain forests, mountains and on the pampas, tobacco, coffee, cocoa, rice and wheat grow abundantly and sub-tropical *junglas* produce an incredible wealth of rare animal and plant life. Incredible wealth is created by the mining of tin, silver and gold.

Situated with its back to the wall of the Andes, Bolivia has, as a result of the misfortunes of war, no outlet to the sea. Even with the expansion of airline traffic it still suffers from economic isolation. Because roads are so bad almost everything imported must come through Chilean or Peruvian ports, or along the railroads of Argentina and Brazil. Not since the golden days that gave my uncle and aunt the affluence they so much enjoyed, has the economy of the country been organized. Revolution has been followed by counter revolution: military juntas succeed one another with brutal monotony. Even as recently as 1946 the bodies of President Villaroel and his Chief of Police were strung up in the Prado outside St Francis's Church in La Paz. Often those who have done most for their country have had to flee overnight for their lives, across the border, and Bolivia, the third largest republic in Latin America, remains the most ignored.

Santa Ana, Cochabamba, Sucre, La Paz – these were the over-familiar names which were always associated with my aunt. Yet somehow I never quite believed that the sounds that rang in my ears were the names of existing places; certainly I felt that when Aunt Jessie died these sounds went with her. It gave me an odd feeling, therefore, to hear the names announced by officials and strangers with the same relish that she gave to the words, and to see 'La Paz' printed on my air ticket. When we looked down from the air at the panoramic view of snow-capped mountains screening the vast, sprawling city, it was like living a fabrication of the imagination: yet this was reality.

We landed at the highest airfield – with the highest casualty rate in the world – on a plateau nearly fourteen thousand feet above sea level. La Paz lay below like a vast crater, with the mountains forming an amphitheatre.

The descent which my aunt describes making by 'brake and fine horses' was made by us in a taxi of perilous age and velocity. Not only was the road carved round the mountain in the most jagged twists, but the traffic seemed to be attempting to defy the laws of gravity, while the giant-size lorries and powerful motor-bicycles tried to overtake each other with a complete disregard of what would be the consequences of a misjudgement of even a few inches. To illustrate the ever-present dangers to the most dare-devil drivers, a completely crumpled car, like a piece of abstract-expressionist sculpture, was exhibited, hoisted on high struts, at one nightmarish corner. This warning was to become a familiar landmark on the many dramatic descents and ascents Sam and I had to make to and from La Paz in every sort of weather, and invariably in a steady stream of wild, antique traffic.

On our initial journey down the mountain, we strained to see the differences between these people and those we had left behind in Peru. The Bolivian women appeared healthier. We noticed the dark plum-coloured glow on their cheeks – as surprising as the fact that the feminine population in rural Japan are often russet-cheeked. Instead of the hard, white hats of the Quechan-speaking women of Peru, they were flaunting, above their pigtails, Andalusian bowler hats of grey and brown. (Frenchwomen would give 'chic' to these odd little hats – not the *mestizo* native; it seems that these must be worn at gauche, 'anti-chic' angles.) These women carry on their backs enormous bundles causing them to lean forward so that their heads are almost at knee-level as they walk; they are capable of covering greater distances, and carrying heavier loads, than their men. Even at the height of the midday sun they wear many layers of thick clothing. Under their flannel ballet skirts there are at least seven or eight heavy petticoats which give the necessary bulk and regulation dimension to their beautiful, bell-like silhouettes. Over their woollen blouses they add at least two coats and a crocheted jacket, and on top of this a shawl. From the folds of a large scarf, tied around their necks, emerges the hand or leg of a sleeping infant. The fact that these women never take off their clothes, even for sanitary purposes, did not bother my aunt; natural dirt was acceptable to Doña Leticia.

In comparison, the men in their ponchos made an insignificant effect. Squat and more than a little ugly, with high Mongolian cheekbones and small, serious eyes, they bore no trace of the beautiful, backward-slanting profile of the Incas.

Already, on the outskirts of La Paz, the street markets began. Under scabrous walls, covered with chalk drawings like the designs of Miro or maladjusted children, old and young women squatted, hopefully rearranging, as if in a chess game, their paltry displays of a few black-spotted fruits, wizened vegetables or cakes, rotting in the sun. The new market stretches like a maze of narrow, gaudy passages; it represents everything that one resents in contemporary life. Nothing is endemic, nothing is what it is meant to be, nothing is pleasing to the eye. As my aunt used to say, it is all 'so much nothing'. Japan has sent her worst taste in poor quality stuffs in plastic, polythene, fibre glass, and every other synthetic substance. The records play Latinized versions of Elvis, 'The Trogs', and 'The Who'; colours are retina-irritant, 'day-glo'. It is a world of hideous trash that can be found in Coney Island, Blackpool, Tangier, Calcutta, Istanbul, or in almost any *souk* throughout the world.

Further down the narrow, steep alleyways, towards the heart of the town, in the old markets, the offerings certainly were more attractive and appetising with richly coloured stuffs, brilliant velvet ballet skirts, boldly patterned ponchos, hand-kerchiefs, scarves, beads, knicknacks and spices.

In these old markets I could appreciate Aunt Jessie's choosing carefully from the displays of parti-coloured rugs, Prince Igoresque blankets of appliqué work and vivid-striped cushion covers. I could visualize her not being able to resist the posies of variegated geraniums and border carnations, and small wild flowers. My aunt became so enraptured by all this colour – the cerises, pinks, scarlets, purples, pea-greens – that it doubtless influenced her into wearing, at King Edward's Drawing Rooms, the court-dresses and trains of magenta, lobster red, purple or black, which made such an impression among the English Irises in the pale-rainbow colours.

Seeing the witch doctors' stalls I could imagine Doña Leticia poking her pudgy little fingers at the dried twigs, and pieces of cork or sulphur. The sprigs of fir and sticks of charcoal were no doubt of benefit for various ailments, and she herself might wish to experiment with an infusion of some of these herbs; but she would be slightly appalled, as indeed we were, by the sight of the llamas' foetuses. The superstitious consider it good luck to bury one of these sinister, shiny black dolls with their spindly bodies, bat-like, bony legs and huge craniums, together with some nail-filings and a hank of hair, under their house if the wife is wishing to give birth to a son and heir. Doña Leticia would have thrown her hands in the air after her first shock and exclaimed: 'Orh, but the poor little things!'

Doña Leticia, on her arrival at this high altitude, would feel, as we did, that delirious sensation which seemed to presage an attack of 'flu, but was, in fact, the *saroche*, or mountain-sickness. Perhaps she suffered from ear-ache or nose-bleeding, and that curious weakness at the back of the knees giving her the impression that her blood had changed to a clear, pale green soup. Certainly, before she became acclimatized to the thin air, she could sleep only fitfully, suffering intermittent night-mares. Doña Leticia, too, would at first, no doubt, be surprised that the lack of oxygen, although it prevents fires, creates a dry-ness so that your wet towels are crisp after being hung up for only a few minutes. It was not to be wondered at that this climate wrought havoc on the delicate complexion of a West-morland blush-rose.

Where did my aunt live in La Paz? I could see her, with her small feet perched on high heels, tottering down the cob-bled lanes between those quite small houses designed origin-ally as dwellings for the aristocracy. They must have been delightful with their patio-gardens and secret-looking façades, but they have long since become slums with eight or ten families living around the inner courtyards, where the wooden balconies and staircases are falling apart, and a white rooster is the chief adornment in the shambles that was once a garden.

The residential area has moved outside the town and is entirely modern. It has all the inhuman cheapness of any garden-city suburb, with low bungaloid buildings of cracked white cement or pebble dash, with picture windows in need of a view, the inevitable spindly, white-painted wrought-iron work, and bulging branches of vulgar bougainvillea: the same sprawling clichés of housing developments almost anywhere in the world today.

Yet a few basic constants remain. La Paz's winter sky is still as cloudless, and of an intensity of blue that makes even

Italian skies seem a pale lapis in comparison, and during the month of July the moon comes up directly behind the snow-spiked summit of the looming Illimani mountain. At nightfall my Aunt Jessie could hear – as we did – the long, sad note of a flute, sometimes accompanied by a drum, and elsewhere a tambourine, beating in a tedious monotonous rhythm.

Hardly had we settled on a round of sightseeing in La Paz, than Sam insisted on a detour to look at Lake Titicaca about which I remembered Aunt Jessie rhapsodizing. Two means of crossing this very large lake are available to the modern traveller: a hydrophoil which takes only a few hours from the Peruvian to the Bolivian shore, and an ancient steamer which has been performing the same slow but gentle service for over a hundred years, and was doubtless the one described by Aunt Jessie in her journal.

We elected to take the hydrophoil to Peru by day, and return by steamer.

The hydrophoil does not give one the best vantage point from which to admire the beauty of the lake, but the journey is made at great speed across the vast stretch of rippleless water. But once aboard the steamer for the return journey Sam and I found ourselves in the last century and able to watch a wonderful, gentle unfolding of marvellous sights. The steamer is today exactly as it was when it was reassembled on this lake in the 1860's. It was made in England in the Victorian style with shiny brass embellishments, upholstery of deep-cut velvet edged with tassels, and lace doilies on arms of chairs and sofas. The beds are brass double-deckers with worn but embroidered linen sheets and faded red velvet covers.

We had been fortunate to get first class tickets for, once all the voyagers had assembled in the dining room, it was evident that there would not be enough cabin-beds to go around. Sure enough, after the meal was over, the dining room was converted into a barracks where the second class passengers were to sleep, while the decks were littered with the sprawling figures of other Indians, with heads resting on their bundles.

At dawn we went on deck; the Indians lay in exactly the same positions they had taken the evening before. The stillness and quiet, as the boat glided slowly, was quite haunting in the opal mist.

Cranes rose into the air with a whir and squawk; diminutive brown Indians in tiny fishing-boats – shaped, as Aunt Jessie most aptly described them, like Turkish slippers – had to hold on tight in our wake. Rising out of the water were strange, pyramid-like islands, black or green, some absolutely symmetrical. Soon the distant silhouette of the Andes became visible and the sun began to rise; then we watched a series of coloured picture postcard effects in the sky.

It was on the shores of this lake that the earliest origins of South American civilization were found. Sea-craft was highly developed by the peoples of Tiahuanaca, and the local papyrus reeds, from which their boats were made, have been found planted in the fresh waters of the islands of the Pacific, proving that these people did not confine their navigation to this sea at the centre of the continent. Papyrus-reed boats were used by the Pharoahs, and are depicted on the palace walls at Nineveh; they have survived in mosaic on the Upper Nile and Lake Chad. It is from their design and material that Thor Heyerdahl built the craft for his romantic and heroic voyages today.

On reaching the shore, we discovered that the Customs officials were as surly as they had ever been. But after our baggage had been completely wrecked, we were finally freed, and a battered taxi took us, past barefoot Indians and herds of llamas, down again into La Paz.

When Don Pedro and his wife moved from La Paz to Sucre or Cochabamba, their journey had to be carefully planned and organized. It was an elaborate procession that, on mule or by horse coach, filed along over precarious bridges, above dangerous rivers, and through narrow mountain gorges and ravines. For compensation, if they were needed, the journey provided a succession of grandiose sights. In the mountain gorges the lakes reflected the sky in sheets of blue glass from which a formation of all-coloured birds would fly at their approach; dwarf blue and white lupins bordered the fields in which women, bowler-hatted and ballet-skirted – an ageless costume – were apparently gesticulating to one another with violent movements of the hands. But they were not using a deaf and dumb language; they were, as they are today, busy with their threads of wool and spool, spinning away, while they tended their flocks or improved each idle moment.

The long months of travel were all part of young Madame Suarez's great adventure, and she would never give a thought to the possibility that here, so far from medical aid, she could be taken ill with an internal flare-up, with stones in the kidneys, a burst appendix, or severe palpitations of the heart.

My aunt always spoke with great respect of the character of the native Indians. She admired them for never losing faith in the Redeemer in the face of all the unalleviated hardships: they knew they would have to suffer these till an early death put an end to their toil and suffering, and hopefully brought them to an easier life. She respected their strange archaic customs: she enjoyed their fêtes and costume carnivals with the devils' masks and elaborate horned headdresses. But Doña Leticia held no belief in the presence of monsters and eerie creatures that were so real in the fanciful minds of the savage; she would not agree that certain parts of the jungle were inhabited by malignant spirits and must never be entered.

For her the forests were nothing short of a paradise of shafts of sunlight filtering through some mottled filigree to fall upon the fronds of giant maidenhair fern, large horizontal leaves of precious gum trees, and cushions of every-textured moss. To my aunt it was all so wonderful that nothing could break the spell of ecstasy. I could imagine her, in her high white choker collar, travelling hat and voluminous petticoats, tramping through the luxuriant undergrowth; but, although the going was difficult, she would be led on. Eventually she would lie down, arms behind her head, the better to gaze up at the cathedral-like vaulting of the green canopy far above. She would watch the endless interplay of lights and shadows through the tracery of the fronds of creepers garlanded from the branches; she would inhale the fragrance from blossom of scented orchids and marvel at the wild fuchsias and the small, spotted gladioli flourishing in the humid, tropic-nurtured growth.

I could visualize her listening to the orchestrated sounds: the twinkling chirps of unknown birds, the yelping of toucans, and the squawk of parakeets. Her ears would be cocked to the concert of the croaking green frogs that lived among the parasitic lichen in the high branches. Then, astonishingly, a deep silence would fall, and it would seem as if the forest were denuded of all its fauna. Then, when again the monkeys started their shrill cackle, their behaviour seemed so comic that Jessie's laughter was added to the general din. Still amused, she would return to the others. 'Chesshie! Where have you been?' Don Pedro would admonish her on the risks she had taken – but Jessie knew better.

Today the air service can cover the same ground as my uncle and aunt in a fraction of the time; yet our air journeys were often uncomfortable and erratic, and seemed to be a battle against logistics. Sometimes, to escape from the long-drawn-out scene in a claustrophobic airport waiting-room, Sam and I wandered out into the sunlight to be faced with the inevitable memorial to some local pilot, with the propeller of his crashed airplane as the centrepiece of a gauche, makeshift shrine. This did not help to boost one's morale for the forthcoming flight, in a very old, battered aircraft, over the tall and jagged mountains where no animal lives.

However, today our pilot had luck on his side – even if his passengers felt that their last unpleasant moments were upon them. After we had been rattled from side to side, and lurched in up-and-downwards bumps, Sam asked me if my hands were sweating as much as his. Yes, they were; but I discovered that whereas I was feeling sick with fright, Sam was merely suffering from the effects on his stomach. A Chinese photographer nearby, judging from his tortured contortions, was suffering from both discomforts. Sam's high spirits and daring, and his raw, sick jokes, sustained me until, with a bad landing, we walked out of the tinny plane to safety and the adventure of discovering Cochabamba, the last outpost of modern civilization we were to see. The formerly grand municipal buildings still looked on to the usual grand square with trees and kiosks, but all were now reduced to a level of the worst contemporary beastliness. Advertisements spread across the streets as in Hong Kong: motor cars and bikes, with throttles open, made an almost deafening volume of sound: even the bicycle bells were of a particularly violent variety. Shops and sidewalk-booths were filled with the sort of goods that could be prizes in a shooting gallery. Our spirits sank as eventually we crossed the bridges over the rivers which bring such fertility to this district, and carried on through to the usual impersonal garden-suburb. Without a church, museum, market or restaurant of interest, Cochabamba, which had held such charm for my aunt, remained an enigma to us and, accepting defeat, we returned to the airport.

We were again following in the tracks of my aunt when we attempted to fly to Sucre. Our erratic progress was straightforward in comparison to my aunt's journey, for travel by land is subject, as we later discovered, to broken bridges, landslides and floods. Electric storms spring up with a surprising violence that is known only in this country; the sudden rages of the sky are terrifying, with zigzag flashes of green and purple. The mountains are obliterated in curtains of driving steel-rod rain; lakes appear where there were none five minutes before, hailstones as large as mothballs bounce off the cobbled alleyways; the gulleys overflowing the streets become gushing rivers; the thunder would even intimidate Wagner.

Our plane to Sucre was delayed by just such a natural event. Surely this sudden thunderstorm which had enveloped Cochabamba would put an end to flying on to Sucre today? No, the Tourist Bureau reassured us, the plane would take off on time; so Sam and I made one more trip to the airport. After several hours' delay, the incessant entreaties to buy dog-eared or stained, out-of-date *Time* magazines brought one back from happier reveries to the horrible reality of wondering how three girls could be as downright repulsive as those Germans sitting together and casting amused – or was it disapproving or lascivious – glances in our direction? One's attention was turned to other unattractive sights: a mongrel with sores, sniffing at the beer spilt from a littered, but abandoned table, a snotty-nosed child with its fly buttons undone, and a group of eight American nuns, who were here to bid adieu to one of their number – a large, loud and full-mouthed girl with her guitar, who had doubtless been the life and soul of many an evening's 'get-together hoot-nanny'.

We had finally reached Sucre. If only we could escape the Customs official and find a vehicle to take us into town! But Sam and I had long since discovered that from no Bolivian airport is there a quick get-away. 'Taxi?' A blank stare. Your luggage is put aboard a dishevelled Chevrolet – one of the two ancient motor vehicles in the region. Then comes the wait. 'Why can't we leave?' Nobody can explain, but at the last moment a half-dozen strangers pile in on top of you. It may be a suitable moment to point out that in the Quechan language there is no word for 'clean'. However, we have no alternative but to welcome our latecomers with good grace. Now the overflowing taxi-cab jettisoned our fellow passengers in various characterless adobe streets, then took us to the further out-skirts of the city to dump us in the empty, ugly hall of a thoroughly depressing hotel, a government-run hostelry and the only accommodation for hundreds of miles. We wondered how, with only a few words of Spanish, we were to set about becoming acquainted with the life of the town.

An energetic, and fortunately most resourceful Spanish maid, with discoloured and gnarled toes emerging from thick, flat sandals, insisted on carrying our heavy luggage to two monastic-looking cells. Then she realized she must further come to our aid. '*Momentito*,' she said as she went to the telephone. 'Mrs Costa will be here at three-thirty,' she later explained and, miraculously, Mrs Costa was.

It is extraordinary that this maid should have been able,

like Aladdin's genie, to produce out of the air the embodiment of our wishes. Mrs de Costa, wearing a hair-do that would have done credit to the most fashionable Paris coiffeur, turned out to be a most delightful *jolie-laide* widow who spoke many languages perfectly, including English, and who not only told us about the churches, monasteries, and museums of Sucre, but could discourse on all aspects of Bolivian life. Comparing existence here today with that in other capitals of the world, she peppered her talk with the names of the latest Paris authors as well as Montaigne, de la Rochefoucauld, and Rousseau, whose pamphlets were much read by South Americans towards the end of the eighteenth century. Mrs de Costa showed neither surprise nor incredulity – for in all things she was a lady.

Mrs Gladys du Rels Costa teaches French at one of the numerous state-run girls' convents, but augments her income by working at the Tourist Bureau. She immediately insisted upon our visiting the imposing, somewhat Austrian-baroque cathedral. It is rich in statues, decorative urns and wrought ironwork, but the *pièce de résistance* is the altar – a sizzling mass of gilt encrustations and guttering candles surrounding the life-size, icon-like painting on wood of the Guadelupe Madonna. Literally thousands of ardent believers have bequeathed their diamonds, emeralds, ropes of pearls, eighteenth-century flower-brooches and nineteenth-century watches to be pinned, wherever space permits, on to the Madonna's triangular skirt. The result is as touching as it is ugly. In a country where the peasant women do not take off their clothes for fear that they be stolen, the fact that never has there been an attempted robbery from this Bolivian Golconda, gave added weight to our impressions. While climbing over the altar to survey the jewels with a magnifying glass, I was positive that my aunt would have been unable to refrain from pinning on to Our Lady one of her pearls, or at least her tubby little gold and enamel watch.

Under expert guidance we came to realize what an important centre Sucre had once been. Its churches are splendiferous, its public gardens give on to a Grand Square, its distinguished buildings rise above lofty arcaded fronts, and rows of grandiose houses are decorated with wrought-iron balconies or exquisite stucco lacework. Innumerable convents with their own imposing chapels were built around huge patios with roof-gardens that command a gigantic panoramic view of turreted rooftops. But Sucre, once so dignified, has become an anachronism, and existence has changed inexorably. The elegant buildings have been converted into small offices and the shops, now of the most lowly nature, appear almost deserted. It is as depressing as anything to be seen in Soviet Moscow. Bolivia at the turn of the century had its poor, but it had its rich; today there are only the poor.

It is perhaps not surprising that the wealthiest families have pocketed their great fortunes and taken them to live in luxury as far away as possible from the land of their birth, since those who have remained where they belong, and have done much to enrich their country as well as themselves, have overnight become the victims of violence – lucky, even if everything has been taken from them, that they have not been tortured or shot. Certainly the native Indian has been the most cruelly exploited of all peoples; but he, in turn, behaves with a signal lack of sympathy for others less fortunate than himself.

With the Agrarian Reform Act of 1952, and its aims to give votes and land to the peasants, the entire economic structure has been changed. All large property owners have been stripped of their land, the tin mines nationalized, and the American Oil Companies confiscated by the State. But the country cannot be said to have benefited, and is still suffering from the effects of shock. The peasants have become disillusioned by promises unfulfilled, there is still no machinery with which to work the land, the supply of minerals is becoming exhausted, and there is little oil. With so many hazards in their way, it is small wonder that outside investors are chary of putting money into the country.

Perhaps it was as well that high altitudes are apt to take away one's appetite, and that ours had not yet returned in the comparative lowlands of Sucre. Coming back for lunch after a five hours' bout of sightseeing, we went expectantly to the restaurant attached to our hotel, the grandest Sucre had to offer. The ceiling was flaking on to the tables which had already been laid out with dried cheese, the cone of salami and slice of tomato, off which some flies were feasting while others had died on the job. Mrs de Costa, a little troubled that we should have remarked unfavourably about our meal, revived hope by extolling the 'lightness' of the food at 'The Polo'. Suffice it to say that, since few people can afford to eat outside their houses today, there is, in this once-great city, not one restaurant where the food is palatable.

After two or three days of near-starvation I found myself conjuring up pictures of chocolate. Surely that frivolous French house with the white baroque decorations must be the fashionable teashop where my aunt had doubtless bought her *gateaux*? Could we perhaps have a cup of chocolate and a piece of pastry? But, since no such thing as fashion exists here, how could such a place succeed? Today, this building-with-a-past deals in refills for tiny electric torches, bicycle clips, or repairs for alarm clocks.

However, one realizes things of quality and innate beauty do still exist when one visits the ancient food and grain market in Tarabuco, fifty miles away, or the miniature market in Sucre. Under canvas awnings those who have brought their produce from the fields sit silently, wearing 'non-colour' natural linens or woven oatmeal-coloured cloths. They make a beautiful entity of browns, buffs, tans. Arranged in golden mounds in front of them is every grade of corn, wheat, rice, maize and saffron. Most spectacular of all are the cone-shaped displays of the potato in all its one hundred and forty varieties, and colours ranging from blue and mauve to rose and yellow. Here the potato, egg-like in shape and peerless in its consistency, bears little resemblance to the often dry-earth-coloured spud of irregular shape which is staple diet at home.

Bustle and noise is a usual ingredient of the market scene, but not here. No voice is raised: no one moves quickly; the place is as muted in sound as it is in colour. Slowly it dawned upon us that it is the coca leaf that produces this lull; the stall owners are quietly chewing the Andean coca leaf, from which cocaine is made. Coca fortifies the system, paralyses the appetite, and enables people to travel incredible distances on foot, or to undertake labours no white man could even attempt. In a haze of happy indifference to the miseries and hardships of their lives they sit without moving until, with monkey-like gesture of a hand, they bring out another anodyne leaf from the little bags in their laps. The coca pellets, which are chewed as tobacco, cause the pupils of the eyes to become so dilated that there is no iris left.

Here in this market we saw one man and wife – Indians from the mountains – wearing unbelievably ragged clothes, with the dirt of ages in their hair and on their sturdy legs. The leather, bonnet-shaped caps on their heads were derived from the Conquistadors' helmet. Physically as beautiful as wild animals, both were of extraordinary strength and energy. Their skins were dark, but their eyes piercingly blue. The woman, submissive and obedient, walked three paces behind her man; the relationship was very basic. The sight of this couple, jungle creatures who could neither read nor write, and whose expressionless hands resembled the claws of a monkey rather than the fingers of civilized man, exuded quite an awesome sense of dignity. They also made one realize that one had indeed travelled to the other end of the universe. Sucre is just about as far away from Europe as one can be; yet, to this couple, Sucre was the great metropolis to be visited perhaps once every five years. Their blue eyes looked around in just the same wonderment as must have those of the young Victorian girl from Westmorland seventy years ago.

Mrs de Costa is nothing if not resilient, and her optimism in all things reminded me of my aunt. She never passes a word of criticism of the way in which her country is being governed, or complaint about the misery to which it is subjected without any hope for the future. Unmentioned was the ever-present menace of Communism. Mrs de Costa has even turned to advantage the change in her own personal fortunes and, with hard work and her powers of adaptability, has become a dominant member of the community. Everyone greets her in the street, many are dependent on her help, and each day brings forth so much of interest that it is difficult for her to keep up with the schedules – yet she found time for us. However, she could not hide her relief when, at last, we left Sucre in the other of the two local cars for a marathon drive to Potosi.

Having driven through the deep gorge through the Andean heights in a haze of dust, we started our ascent to the silver-mining town fourteen thousand feet above sea level. Our car smelt stiflingly of petrol fumes as it banged and bounced at great speed round the spiralling bends in the mountains. Suddenly an ear-splitting sound of screeching brakes was augmented by the screams from the Cholo women in the on-coming bus as they clapped their hands over wide-open mouths. We avoided a head-on collision with an inch to spare between the wheels and the precipice.

A group of Indians, who had dismounted from another bus and were having a saffron-coloured meal at a roadside tavern, first warned us of danger ahead. The rains had caused an avalanche. We sought advice from everyone we passed as to whether to continue or not. After trying our luck and forging forward for an hour, we came to a halt. The driver got out and went ahead on foot to investigate, while Sam and I sat with our legs dangling in a gushing mountain stream. The driver returned with the inevitable negative: the *camino* was impassable. The alternative to remaining in an Indian café for three days and nights was what Aunt Jessie called an about-turn.

Our spirits were low on the way back to Sucre. We regretted not having followed my aunt up the tortuous, narrow streets of Potosi which, in its days of glory, the guide-book told us, boasted sixty churches in addition to the superb Matriz cathedral. Today, apparently only half a dozen churches remain, some of which have been turned into cinemas; but in spite of change and decay there are still baroque arcaded plazas, triumphal columns and pinnacles, and the Mint built in the fourteenth century. Photographs show that Potosi still possesses some of the finest examples of colonial architecture with the most fanciful decoration: carved in stone with the delicacy of shell work are grotesque masks, double-headed falcons, sun-burst heads, and personages in elaborate Elizabethan costume.

We were disappointed not to return with the beakers, pitchers, ewers and bowls of heavy Potosi silver of which my aunt made such a collection. Most disappointing of all, we had not been able to visit the mines. Although conditions have improved, it would have been an illuminating if harrowing ex-perience to see the way in which human beings are still forced to earn a scant livelihood. For someone like my aunt, with such an acute gift for compassion, they were always a shocking sight. Her letters home were filled with exclamation marks of disgust as she described the miners, half-naked and sweating, working inhumanely long shifts in a foetid, poisonous atmos-phere which led irrevocably to a painful, early death. But, by degrees, she came to accept – like the native himself – that life for the Indian is one of ceaseless toil, which he himself has grown to accept as his destiny. He acknowledges that his degre-dation will end only on that inevitable day when the white man decides to leave the continent, bequeathing it to those to whom it belongs by right, and who, alone, know how to battle against its enigmatic odds and mysteries.

Arriving back late at our unloved hotel in Sucre, we ate the remains of the sandwiches Mrs de Costa had provided for our picnic lunch. They tasted of petrol fumes.

Once more we had to rely upon the imagination of Mrs de Costa for our diversions during the two days before the next plane to Cochabamba and civilization. We found her in her old family house which she considers herself extremely fortunate still to live in, even though she must let out most of it to lodgers. Whereas her grandfather had seventeen servants, she has only one (a toothless hag who prepared those particularly appetite-repellent sandwiches for us). Mrs de Costa could easily trans-plant herself to a luxurious life acting as hostess to her father who, having been for years Bolivian Ambassador to France (where his daughter was brought up), is now his country's representative at UNESCO. But Mrs de Costa loves Sucre. It has always been an intellectual centre, with its famous university, its aristocratic families renowned for their taste and manners and refined way of life, and the administrative authorities, working here for the whole of the *alti-plano*. Mrs de Costa realizes how much circumstances have changed, but prefers to remain where she feels she belongs and can be of help.

16 Disclosure

During the first day's tour of Sucre I had told Mrs de Costa of my links with Bolivia. She was intrigued. 'Then perhaps you knew Mr Urriolagoitia?' she asked. Indeed I remembered Urrio, as my aunt referred to him, a man with dark shadows under his long, languorous eyes, who had become bald at a very early age. He had a thumb missing as a result of using a loaded gun as a walking-stick. Urrio was, as my aunt said, 'a cut above' the other Secretaries in the Legation.

'He became our President, you know.'

'Was he a good one?'

'Oh yes, excellent.'

'But they kicked him out after four years, didn't they?' I queried.

'Yes, they always do.'

I asked Mrs de Costa if I might be allowed to call upon this old friend who I was confident would remember me as well as I remembered him. A little later, Mrs de Costa, having been on the telephone, informed me that Mamerto Urriolagoitia remembered me very well – and that I was, at that early age, a promising painter. He would have liked to see me again, but unfortunately he was not getting dressed today: he had not been at all well. I asked: 'What age is he?' The reply that he was eighty came as a shock. I later heard that Urrio had become the Patriarch of Sucre and was greeted everywhere with welcoming cries of 'Mamerto'. He had become extremely deaf, and was finding the disadvantages of old age very difficult to bear.

When we now met again, and Mrs de Costa (a most resourceful cicerone) started us off on another sightseeing tour, she explained that she had been in contact with several people still living here who knew my aunt well in her Sucre day. One eminent lady invited us to see her collection of early photographs including some of Madame Suarez; two widowed sisters living together would also like very much to talk about their memories of her.

In the Museum of Decorative Arts I was impressed by a display of native costumes shown on a collection of dolls; but it was while we were wandering down a gallery devoted to portraits of Bolivian personalities that I saw, even larger than life – and in life she was a vast enough woman, in fact a giantess among a race of near-pygmies – a full-length oil portrait, dated 1899, of none other than Princess Glorietta. 'And who the hell is Princess Glorietta?' Sam asked.

I cannot say that, as a boy just able to walk, I had ever truly met this lady, but I knew her well by sight for she became a great friend of my aunt. Indeed the photograph groups of the swarthy princess with the sulky, proud expression and the choker of solitaire diamonds, squatting in the company of Mamita Aramayo and my aunt, had been an early source of wonder. Although there are no titles in the Republic, certain South Americans have been known, in recognition of their contribution to the Vatican, to be given honours by the Pope. Princess Glorietta was a member of the rich Alcantara family, and her donation had obviously been a suitably fat one.

It was now time for us to pay the call, arranged by Mrs de Costa, on one of my aunt's former friends, Madame de Zelada. This was the elderly lady who had made and dressed those museum dolls we had admired earlier. On arrival at Madame de Zelada's house, we waited in a small salon which was both Spanish and French in its formality. The spindly chairs and sofa were stiff and hard; above the doors and windows were extremely ornate wooden pelmets from which hung yellow silk curtains; old family photographs in elaborate, over-bright gilt frames were hung on the otherwise bare plastered walls. A door opened, giving a glimpse of a room cluttered with books and papers in which St Jerome might have studied, and Madame Maria Urioste de Zelada appeared. She had a hauntingly beautiful but tragic face, with deep-set, dark eyes

and white silky hair, with ivory hands that now were as tremb-
lingly articulate as those of a hysterical Greco saint.

Yes, Madame de Zelada told us, she had known well the
beautiful Madame Suarez. I may have appeared somewhat
surprised.

'You know, don't you, that your aunt was very beautiful?'
she asked.

As children we had not considered her so: she was too
small, and too plump and painted. But now I could understand why, in this country where most women are short and
sallow, Aunt Jessie, with her incandescent complexion, even
in her later years, must have been extremely striking.

'She had such a perfect nose – her profile was pure
Etruscan – altogether such beautiful features!'

Madame de Zelada had been a young girl when my Uncle
Percy had, in spite of his 'disgrace' in England, been promoted
by ex-President Ismael Montes to Prefect of the Department
of Chuquisaca towards the end of the First World War. The
Liberal party in Bolivia had been in power for nearly twenty
years, and no one had risen to challenge the influence of the
twice-President Montes until the party tried to gain re-election
for a sixth period. One of the candidates then nominated for
the Presidency was Don Pedro Suarez, but his chances were
wrecked by the revolution which put the Republicans in power.
Yet, surprisingly, it was Don Pedro who acted as mediator between the two warring Republican leaders. It must have given
great satisfaction to my aunt to realize that her husband was so
highly considered in his own country.

Once again Madame Suarez was an official hostess and,
since she was so fond of young people, Madame de Zelada had
been invited a great deal to the house. Yes, my aunt had lived
for, it must be, fifteen years on the nearby Nicholas Ortiz
Street. Although by then middle-aged, she often played tennis
with Madame de Zelada, and afterwards they would go back for
a litle party, which developed into a big party – for life in my
aunt's house seemed to be one long carousal.

Madame de Zelada now brought out two large plastic
bags filled with carefully preserved souvenirs: reproductions

of the Certificate of Independence of Bolivia, mementoes of Royal visits, and, dating back into the early 'eighties, groups of local ladies in high-camp fancy dress. Here was a concertina folder of waxwork-stiff portraits of all the Presidents of Bolivia: a pretty comic galaxy they made, with vast moustachios, baroque beards and frenetic hair styles. Some were extremely ferocious: all wore orders and decorations displayed upon pouter-pigeon chests. Yes, here was Mamerto Urriolagoitia and, in spite of the long, black, pointed beard, easily recognizable with his bald, egg-shaped head and big, shadowy eyes. A menacing stare replaced the languorous regard of his youth. His uniform was heavy embroidered in gilt, and he wore with obvious pride the grand blue ribbon of the Order of the Condor of the Andes across his chest. Since those early days under my uncle's wing, Urrio had done well for himself. A scholar and courageous traveller (he went with the writer, Julian Duguid, through the 'Green Hell' of the Paraguayan jungle), he was appointed Consul-General in England. On returning to Bolivia he became Vice-President and when, unexpectedly, the young President was taken ill and retired, Urrio's position was the first in the land. Near the end of his term of office, he agreed with the army to transfer the government to a military junta. A few months later, the Nazi-inspired Estensorro party rebelled against the junta and overthrew the government with a revolution that reduced La Paz to a blood-bath.

Other friends or relations of Madame de Zelada who had achieved grandeur in the Diplomatic Corps were stiffly photographed together in their gilt-embroidered court uniforms. Here was a quartet of strangely contrasting characters, old and young, thin and fat, distinguished and not so distinguished. The group celebrated the occasion when the Bolivian Minister in London left his residence at 102 Cromwell Road to present his credentials to Queen Victoria at Windsor Castle; from left to right: Alberto Gutierrez, Francesco Argandana, and the Minister, Feliz Avelino Aramayo. Looming over his shoulder was a very large and dark-eyed military attaché with dagger-like moustachios, the young Pedro Suarez. The photograph had been taken before I was born, when my uncle was first married. By what strange decree of fate, I wondered for the thousandth time, had my aunt's choice alighted upon this particular man?

'Here we are – here is your aunt,' and Madame de Zelada's ivory fingers laid down a large cardboard-backed 'Portrait by Lanfier, London' of a very young girl in full court dress. The picture, dated 1899, and inscribed for her friend the sultry Princess Glorietta, '*de su sincera amiga,* Leticia de Suarez,' showed the somewhat awed sitter in Prince of Wales feathers, tiara, and diamond necklace, in a dress of flowered brocade and a fur-topped, ruched cape with stand-up Elizabethan collar. Her white kid-gloved hands were very gingerly placed, one on her lap and one on a brocade-covered table on which some variegated grasses sprouted from an epergne. The whole effect was archaic, yet something about the gravity of this wide-eyed girl was extremely touching. Yes, she was beautiful. I had not seen this particular photograph before, although the groups taken at the same sitting were like familiar friends as they were now presented to me once more. Here was my aunt, the military attaché's wife, sitting with the large, lolling Princess Glorietta, while the Minister's wife, the frail Madame Aramayo, in black sequins and appliqué flowers, stood between them. In an alternative pose my aunt stood while the Princess continued to more than occupy a chair. Many members of the Aramayo family had remarked upon the lack of etiquette and had scolded the older lady for not insisting that she too, as the wife of the Minister, should have been provided with a seat. It seemed curious that here, half a world away, was the same photograph which for years has graced a table in the drawing room of my Wiltshire house. But the dry, crystalline air of Sucre had preserved the print in the pristine condition in which it must have left the photographer's dark room; my photographs at home have acquired a slightly sepia glaze.

Mrs de Costa had still other cards to play: she would now table in the drawing room of my Wiltshire house. But the dry, years. The address was in what had once been a residential district of quiet distinction. The façade of Aunt Jessie's house, built within a yard of the street with tall, shuttered windows and balconies, was coral-painted. We went through the large, formal front door with, above it, a coloured-glass window, slightly reminiscent of West Hampstead. One saw that the house was built around a patio with arched columns. The effect was somewhat bare and austere; calla lilies and cannas, in separate L-shaped beds among the paving stones of the court-yard, were a mere condescension of a garden. High on the opposite wall was a most unexpectedly large and elaborate window, quite out of keeping with the classical Empire style of the rest. It was only when the present owner of the house, a grey-haired woman in a grey tubular dress, with a long, toothy smile, welcomed us upstairs, that we saw the felicities of this modest-sized, but cheerful country house in town. Our hostess gave the date of the building as 1875. Here above the patio were the living rooms and bedrooms, airy and light, designed to ward off summer's heat. On seeing the salon I immediately realized that little could have been changed since my aunt's day. Here, so recognizable, was the same taste that my aunt displayed in the drawing room at Compayne Gardens. The chairs were placed in twos against the walls, or formed solitary islands on the elaborately patterned red and pink carpet. The false 'Louis-style' suite of chairs and sofa were here made of a black wood and upholstered in crimson and buff imitation Aubusson. In a corner stood a marquetry cabinet with glass front to protect the display of questionable china ornaments. The yellow silk curtains, drawn against the ravages of the sun, were topped by much-too-heavy pelmets. I knew of old that the gilt table with its large bowl of splayed-out gladioli had always been placed in the centre of the room. All that was missing were the knicknacks and my aunt's melodious laughter.

But even more interesting was the dining room. Certainly this can have changed even less since the Prefect's wife had given her gastronomic feasts here. The heavy mahogany reproduction furniture might have been ordered *en suite* from a Sears and Roebuck or Maples catalogue in the 'seventies: it was heavy, ornate, shiny, brown-leather covered. The dining table could be made – with extra leaves – to stretch to the sideboard with its cathedral-pinnacles, at the far end of the room; around the walls were the stiff rows of chunky-looking chairs awaiting the arrival of greedy-gut guests. The carpet was brown, and the velvet curtains at the windows and doors, in such good condition, were also brown and embroidered with scrolls and arabesques. They brought back to my mind what I had forgotten – the curtains in the hall of my earliest childhood house in Langland Gardens. I *knew* that these had been Aunt Jessie's, and they were in as perfect condition today as when they were first ordered.

The room had been expressly designed for the enjoyment of good meals: it filled such a purpose perfectly. It was as ugly as only the best old-fashioned restaurants can have been in Vienna or Brussels. Thanks to the large art nouveau window, which we had noticed from the courtyard, the room was now basking in a flood of sunlight which poured through the swirling glass panes on to the brown on brown on brown.

I could easily envisage my aunt here. In her flowing dressing-gown she would go out into the servants' quarters, the pantries and the kitchens where the shelves went high to the ceilings, and where the storage cupboards, cooking ranges and large stoves might have been those of a well-equipped restaurant. In these large rooms she would examine with great curiosity the latest purchases from the market. She would appraise the fruits, pinch the chicken breasts, and arrange the tuberoses in tall, trumpet-shaped vases. Then in good time she would start to prepare her appearance. This was the epoch when her hair was worn in a tight-waved cone with a large Spanish kiss curl over each ear. Her hair was now dyed a deep mahogany red, her white complexion made whiter with liquid powder. She would put on a champagne-coloured tussore dress embellished with guipure embroidery, and the heels of her tiny white kid shoes were of scarlet patent-leather. Now she was welcoming the guests, apologizing for the late appearance of Pedro, and attempting to 'keep the ball rolling merrily'. Soon she was sending everyone off into gales of laughter: 'a perfect scream,' 'a donkey,' they called her as she dominated the scene.

Don Pedro would arrive last. The banquet was

announced, and the countless servants, in their sandalled feet, started running to and from the large nether-quarters nearby. For a major portion of the afternoon they would be bringing in course after course of highly seasoned dishes: the fishes from Lake Titicaca, the *chunias* (very hard to chew, but a great favourite) with curried eggs, the *empanadas,* and the chickens with the *arroz a la Valenciana.* How they managed without ice and with so little refrigeration I don't know, but no doubt some means were invented to make the sorbet before the *pièce de résistance* of marinated pork. After the desserts the fruits brought with them all the exoticism of the jungle.

Mrs de Costa now had her trump card to play with our visit to the two widowed sisters, the Mesdames Esther Urioste Villa and, ten years younger, Clothilde Urioste Benavides. The sisters' house was furnished with more individuality and a greater number of relics of former wealth than the others we had seen. The corridors were lined with high-backed, eighteenth-century walnut chairs of special charm. There were vistas, through columns, of standard rose-trees and rambling, straggly flowers in a small patio garden, and glimpses of a bedroom, with the inevitable llama fur rug on the large brass bed; souvenirs dotting the walls were a mixture of sixteenth-century Spain and Edwardian England. The dining room, brown and white, had slight overtones of Vermeer, and it was obvious that the sisters had, apart from their possessions, acquired a lifestyle of sophistication.

Perhaps in Bolivia it has always been considered necessary to conform to the strictest formality in the furnishing of the room where guests are received; otherwise, how could one explain, in this otherwise delightful house, why, in the salon, no vestige of individuality was to be discovered? On the day of our sudden visit it was not looking its best for the chairs, placed in rows against the walls, were hidden under white dust-covers, except for a sample sofa-chair displaying the intricacy of the hand-worked embroidery of delicate convolvulus and tendrils in biscuit colour on blue silk. Overpowering gilt frames did honour to unworthy painted porcelain plaques, much too high on the walls. Again the sultry Princess Glorietta glowered from above. This time, as well as the usual stomacher of diamonds, the ubiquitous millionairess was accoutred in a huge chinchilla cape.

The Mesdames Urioste, one with cropped white hair and black *tailleur,* and the other in smart Paris grey, were a little incongruous in this setting. Completely contemporary in their points of view, their desire to glance back at the past showed itself solely in their wish to talk to me of Doña Leticia. They seemed so pleased at this rare opportunity; they had obviously made their decisions about which aspects of their friendship they were anxious to emphasize. It was Clothilde, the younger sister, who declared:

'What we admired and respected about your aunt was her purity – her purity of spirit – or could you say her soul?'

'Yes, that was it,' nodded the elder sister. 'She had a very pure soul.'

This was unexpected. Although I was pleased, I was again surprised. I had imagined these friends would admire my aunt's high spirits, her sense of fun, and her ability to make everybody laugh, with and at her. I had expected them to talk of her more frivolous aspects; but these sisters were right: it was indeed this simplicity, this basic goodness, that, in spite of all her extravagances of manner, had made her indispensable to many. It was nice to hear the tribute to the soundness of her character, her generosity and kindness, upon which the two ladies were now embarked. It was good to hear again how much her religion meant to her, and how she was always helping people – not only those who came to the house with some insoluble problem, or with perhaps only a request for money, but those she met at church or in the convent who seemed to want just to be around, and to receive comfort and happiness in her presence. In the Nicholas Ortiz house, it seemed, there were many old people just sitting in the corridors. Perhaps they had once worked for her, and were now too frail to do so; yet she could never be rid of them. I remembered, back in England, that marvellous old Indian cook, Isabel

Villegas, whom she had looked after until her end; I remembered the Sisters of Mercy sitting in the hall in the light of the coloured stained-glass window.

'But do tell me,' I asked, 'how did my aunt strike you as a personality? Did you find her unconventional, flamboyant?'

'Flamboyant, oh no!' interjected Esther the elder; 'she was too elegant for that. She was extremely elegant.'

'Tremendously dressy,' added Esther, 'always something one had never seen! And her entertainments! They were wonderful, and she entertained all the time: every day there was a reception!'

I laughed.

'They knew the best in the land!'

The Urioste sisters were enjoying their voyage into the past, with many forgotten memories coming to the surface, reminding them of my aunt's 'Merry Widow' hats, her bridge parties, and the latest arrivals from abroad.

I then told these ladies of my aunt's poverty later in life and asked whether, after the Casa Suarez debacle, my uncle and she had seemed to want for money when living in Sucre?

'Oh no! They lived in luxury. All the while they were here they seemed to be very lavish. They had dozens of servants.'

I was glad to know that the financial pinch had not yet become serious.

The elder sister announced: 'Doña Leticia was always so lively, and interested in many things. She was wonderful at telling fortunes with the cards – but better with the palm of the hand. And she sang. . . .'

I considered it time to bring in a little contrast to this valentine to my aunt. 'I remember her moaning Tosti's "Goodbye For Ever" dreadfully off-key, like an old cow in the extremes of pain. "Caterwauling" my mother called it.' Laughter. 'And her Spanish? Could she speak fluently?'

'Yes. In those days so few English ever bothered to speak any language but their own. But her accent was perfect, and she was always so polite. In answer to invitations from friends she would say: "*Muy bien, estaremos encantades de verlos.*"

(Thank you very much, we will be enchanted to see you.)'

'But her French had a strong English accent: it always made us laugh.'

More laughter. Sister Clothilde now came to my aunt's defence. 'And she was very proficient at tennis. There was an Australian "pro" who taught us all, and she became very skilled and entered into all the competitions.' Esther, too, remembered that my aunt was always encouraging the very young to come to her house; she loved young people.

'When she employed two young sisters as housekeeper and dressmaker, her friends warned her that, knowing her husband's weakness for a pretty face, she was asking for trouble. But Doña Leticia would not hear a word against the latest addition to the household. The dresses the elder sister made were every bit as good as Paris, and the younger girl, who became a sort of *dame de compagnie,* taught her all that she was to learn about cooking. But it was this girl who brought Doña Leticia's marriage to an end.'

Never had there been a whisper in our household that Jessie's marriage had broken up; I had heard vaguely from my mother that Uncle Percy died, penniless, of a broken heart. The diffidence or secrecy – whatever you like to call it – with which personal matters at home were discussed was surely very exceptional – if not downright peculiar?

'They had a marital separation,' said Clothilde.

'Yes,' repeated Esther, 'a marital separation. It was not only that the girl was so very young but, as your aunt remarked: "I wouldn't care if only he'd go out of the house to do it." Eventually the girl and your uncle did a midnight flit and settled in La Paz.'

'The insatiable old goat!'

'Your aunt remained here in the Rue Nicholas Ortiz; but eventually she decided she could not put up with the situation any longer.'

'Very few South American women ever leave their husbands, however unfaithful they are, but Doña Leticia decided she had had enough.'

'Since Don Pedro was sending her no financial support,

she decided to sell a very beautiful diamond ring, and with this she paid for her return to England.'

A new pang of sympathy for my aunt ran through me at the realization that the gamble of her marriage had not, after all, been a success. She had returned, in late middle-age, a discarded, childless wife, with her black diamonds and black pearls, her plait of seed pearls and her tiara as her worldly legacy.

I realized now that it was later, during a children's party for my sisters at Temple Court, when the jellies in half-oranges had been finished, and we were all dancing Sir Roger de Coverly, that a telegram had arrived. As the last of the guests in Shetland shawls had been seen out, my aunt was noticed hurrying up to her room in a flood of tears.

No questions were asked, and no explanation was given as to why, for a year, Aunt Jessie wore only the deepest black. Now it transpired that Uncle Percy had lived on in La Paz dissipating the relics of his fortune. His death from pneumonia was not the violent one that had been for so long expected.

While Uncle Percy had doubtless upset and shocked my aunt by his infidelities, she never gave a hint of criticism to others, and no doubt felt great remorse that she had not remained nearby to nurse him at the end. She lived with the secret of her disillusion and broken marriage unmentioned, and always spoke of 'Peth-er-orh' as a pillar of strength.

Aunt Jessie had become to me suddenly a rather different character: perhaps not a tragic one, but with a background of sorrow to the façade of gaiety that she showed at all times even to those closest and dearest. I came away from the two Urioste sisters glad that, at last, I realized her hidden depths; no doubt, that was why her frivolities never appeared just empty. Now I could see that they sprang from an understanding of the contrasts of life, and the need to appear to the world with a brave face. I could suddenly hear the pathos in her voice and in her laughter.

Today the number of people who remember my aunt has dwindled. Most of them have themselves become old, and their memories are vague and even conflicting. But whenever the subject of Aunt Jessie is mentioned, even though to describe never-to-be-forgotten impressions is not easy, I notice that, however tired or aged or ill her survivors may be, at the thought of her their faces always light up with a smile of affection and amusement.